ACHIEVING
LIFETIME
EMPLOYABILITY

ACHIEVING LIFETIME EMPLOYABILITY

Principles
Performance
Perception
Politics

ASHOK SHAH, G. ROSS KELLY,
and DILEEP SRINIVASAN

gatekeeper press

Columbus, Ohio

The Four P's: The Keys to Achieving Lifetime Employability

Published by Gatekeeper Press
2167 Stringtown Rd, Suite 109
Columbus, OH 43123-2989
www.Gatekeeperpress.com

ISBN 9781642376661

Printed in the United States of America

Dedication

We always recognize soldiers, firemen, and policemen for their services to protect us. We seldom hear, talk or acknowledge the services of **Caregivers** for their selfless dedication and pursuit in bringing people back towards normalcy.

In the span of our careers, we encounter various obstacles and hardships, that only with the help of our family and caregivers, are we able to recover and get back in the race.

Our pursuit of lifetime employability is highly dependent on their tireless effort, dedication and services.

We dedicate this book to **Caregivers of the world** . . . as they are the unsung heroes in our careers and our health.

Testimonials

In their latest book, *Achieving Lifetime Employability,* Ashok Shah and his co-authors continue to be thought provoking. Their previous book, *The 'Me' Enterprise,* is one of the most influential professional book that I have read in the last 10 years. The Life@Persistent program was strongly influenced by the book and we have designed our internal processes to help individuals take ownership of their personal lives and professional careers. With *Achieving Lifetime Employability,* the authors have gone one step further to provide the 4P framework of Principles, Performance, Perception and Politics. This book builds on *The Me Enterprise* to provide very practical tips from which to build a successful and fulfilling career.

—Dr. Anand Deshpande, Founder, Chairman, Managing Director - Persistent Systems Limited

Lifetime employability is something every employee aspires to achieve. And in the ever-changing, fast paced 21st century, that is becoming increasingly difficult. If there is such a thing as a roadmap, *Achieving Lifetime Employability* may be it. This is something every employee, of any age or any position, should have in their hip pocket.

—Dr. Diane Hamilton, Author and Syndicated Radio Host

To remain relevant, employees must demonstrate agility and adaptability. Achieving Lifetime Employability provides that understanding in terms of how to contribute value to organizations in the midst of rapid changes in technological and competitive landscapes is a mandate for anyone who wants to have enduring relevance in the workplace.

—Dr. Cynthia Newman, Dean College of Business Administration Rider University

The lifetime employability is the key issues of the day. This book is a must read for anyone who wants to have a sustained fulfilling lifetime career unimpeded by changes all around us. As a C-level employee at several companies I have learned hard way the lessons which this book provides.

—Dr. Siddhartha Dalal Professor of Practice,
Columbia University

In world where continuous learning is the only way to continue to be impactful, this book creates a framework along the multiple dimensions we have to grow.

—Nigel Vaz CEO, Publicis Sapient

The insights shared in *Achieving Lifetime Employability* are relevant, practical, and powerful for anyone wishing to build a remarkable career. As our marketplace continues to grow in complexity and uncertainty, the principles contained in the book can help guide each one of us to a fulfilling career of lifelong learning and tremendous opportunity.

—David A. Esposito, Managing Partner,
Harvest Time Partners, Inc.

In coaching Millennials and other mid-level employees, I am constantly asked 'what is the secret to getting ahead and staying ahead in the workplace?' If you are a leader that is focused on performance, *Achieving Lifetime Employability* is a must read to help you on the road to success!

—Becky Thomas
Author and Next Generation Coach™

In their recent publication, *Achieving Lifetime Employability*, the authors provide valuable advice on how to navigate the complex terrain of the 21st century Corporation. The evaluation models they provide are smart, sensible, and substantive, as they detail the critical attributes required to be an attractive contributor in the workplace.

> *—Kannankote 'Sri' Srikanth New Ventures Advisor and former Corporate Executive*

Authors Kelly, Shah, and Srinivasan take a different approach to achieving business success, developing your personal skills, adjusting, honing, focusing on your value to your employer, current and future. Always adding value as a self-preservation proposition.

They have experienced challenges and success in the highly competitive and highly technical business world, through evolution of the PC, the internet, the cloud and through AI and IOT, and have now captured their learnings in one concise package. The lessons are the same. Read it. Do it.

> *—Jim Neil Senior Project/Program Manager*

Your goal is to win the war not the battle, throughout your career you will have many battles that can cause you to fall off course and erode your career objectives. This book provides a framework to stay the course and keep your sights on the overall objective of winning the war or improving your brand to reach the level in your career you sought out to achieve".

> *—Guy DelGrande Chief Executive Officer Tekmark Global Solutions*

Lifetime employability was the norm when my parents worked for GM in Detroit in the 1950's. GM's market share in those days was 53%. Fast forward to 2019, GM's market share is 17%, and plenty of downsizing, rightsizing and workforce reductions have accompanied that decrease.

In contrast to my parents, my career has consisted of twenty + years of mergers, acquisitions, buy-outs and similar reductions. Welcome to the world of self-reliance.

As *Achieving Lifetime Employability* so clearly describes, I and everyone else in the 21st century workforce is responsible for their own employability. Fortunately, for the reader, the book also explains what to do to achieve and sustain it.

—Clint Cuny Director and CEO, North American Operations
Techno Brain

The Greek aphorism *Know Thyself* is at least as relevant today as it was back in ancient times. The collection of ten quotients, 4P›s and Balanced Quotient Scorecard tools enable all of us to focus on the things that *really* matter in order to truly know ourselves, and enable us to not only achieve, but to thrive, throughout our lifetime of employability.

—Dr. Vik Muiznieks
Director, Technology Innovation and Integration
MIT Lincoln Laboratory

Contents

Foreword

Less than three months after publishing *The Emergence of the 'Me' Enterprise,* we were confronted with what numerous authors encounter, embodied in the expression:

"The instructions make more sense after the bicycle has been put together."

Following the book's publication, we embarked on the obligatory series of reviews, talks, interviews and discussions with audiences from colleges, major universities, corporations and civic clubs. We were pleasantly surprised—elated, in fact—with the feedback we received from readers. The reviews were excellent. We knew almost instantly we had struck a chord with those who were in leadership roles, those who were aspiring leaders, and those who were just beginning their careers. The "Blueprint" was working.

We also received, however, feedback that various segments in the book begged for more explanation, more elaboration. Readers were very complimentary about how the "Blueprint" provides a foundation for surviving and thriving in the 21st century. But they had more questions. Readers applauded our ability to take the many divergent elements that are critical to employability and leadership, and put them into a single, logical framework. But they asked for more elaboration.

They told us how, for the first time in their careers, they felt they had a roadmap to keep their careers viable. But they asked for more. They provided real examples of the value they received, and they asked questions . . . more questions than time would allow us to answer.

We knew we had created something meaningful for those in search of how to establish and maintain their leadership edge in the new age of employment where seniority was no longer enough. They wanted more.

There was certainly more that we could say, but could we structure it into book form and make it equally compelling for the reader?

Having collected our thoughts, inputs and learnings from our experiences in writing, publishing and speaking about the *'Me' Enterprise*, we had to ask ourselves: do we have enough meaningful content to write a follow-up book? Is there more we could say that would be additive to 'the blueprint for leadership', yet not be redundant? The answer, we concluded, was an overwhelming "yes". Can we provide that information in a clear, concise and memorable framework, similar to the "Blueprint" model we provided in our last book? Again, we concluded, "yes, we can". Finally, we asked ourselves, is there a perspective that we should provide in a second book that we might not have in the *'Me' Enterprise*? Is there a viewpoint that we may be missing that can be provided from another angle, perhaps from another professional who is a thought leader on the topic of leadership in the digital age, and had new ideas and a different vantage point?

If two heads were better than one in constructing the *'Me' Enterprise*, could three heads be better than two in our efforts to write a follow-up book? Again, the answer was "yes", especially if that third head is the caliber of Dileep Srinivasan!

Like Ashok and me, Dileep has been through the wars. As the Farmers Insurance commercial says, *He knows a thing or two because he's seen a thing or two.* That is what comes with over thirty years of experience in the IT services and consulting industry, all the while monitoring and tracking the emerging role of digitization in the workplace. From the ground floor to executive and partnership positions, Dileep has established himself as a thoughtful leader and visionary, and offers a perspective that we concluded would indeed be beneficial.

From the collective viewpoint of Ashok, Dileep and myself, we humbly offer you what we believe is the newest paradigm that will serve as a roadmap to leadership in the age of digitization, disruption and transformation.

That roadmap begins with a series of assumptions that will guide us through this publication:

The Elephant in the Room

With this book, we began where we left off with our previous publication. In the latter half of the 20th century, many countries experienced exceptional growth and prosperity. Companies large and small contributed to and enjoyed that prosperity, as did their employees. That prosperity, however, also created an expectation that lingers even today.

Many of our parents and grandparents began and ended their careers with the same company. They experienced lifetime employment and when they retired, they were rewarded with anything from a gold watch to a lucrative pension plan.

Lifetime employment, if not the norm, was certainly the expectation and desired outcome of many people's careers. In some cases, it was even promised.

Then everything changed.

With the advent of the Internet, global competition and the technology revolution, companies and industries began experiencing cost issues. "Corporate reengineering" became the buzzword. To offset their growing infrastructures, companies began initiating cost reduction actions, ranging from downsizing to restructuring and changing compensation plans. Gone were the company cars. Gone were the unlimited expense accounts. First class travel became business class. Business class became Coach. The perks were gone, and in some cases, so were the jobs.

In the midst of it all, however, the assumptions of lifetime employment remained.

Even though the harsh realities were staring them in the face suggesting otherwise, those who began their careers pre-Internet, held tightly to that notion. When it came time for the hard discussions about layoffs, cost reductions and changes to employment and compensation plans, the concept of lifetime employment became the elephant in the room that no one wanted to discuss.

What about your commitment to your employees? What about the loyalty we gave you all those years? In the face of those uncomfortable questions, employers simply looked at their shoes and meekly apologized.

Even today, knowing the possibility of lifetime employment with the same company is no more assured than the stock price of internet start-up's, there are still those who cling to the notion. That elephant in the room, while referenced in our previous book, has taken center stage to become the singular focus of this publication.

How do we change our mindset from the notion of lifetime employment to one of a new paradigm . . . lifetime employability? How do we maintain our knowledge, our skillset, our very relevance in the workplace, in the face our own aging, changing values and cultures, and drastic innovations in technology? How do we prove and re-prove our value in new competitive environments and new companies? How do we continue to reinvent ourselves as the companies and the world around us continue to change, and the value that proved us to be worthy of hiring in our last company ten years ago, is no longer relevant?

Those and other questions are our focus for this publication.

A Framework for Lifetime Employability

Successful leaders and employees of all types and positions do not function based on buzzwords, fads or catchphrases. Instead, their success tends to center around what we've concluded are the *Four P's:*

- *Principles* that guide their actions and behaviors;
- *Performance* that is reliable and congruent with those principles;
- *Perception,* how you project yourself and are perceived others; and

- *Politics,* how you navigate the political machinations of your organization.

From college interns to "C" level executives, it is those same four P's that consistently differentiate the highly successful from their peers. It is those characteristics that define effective leaders in today's environment, and, it is those same characteristics that are essential for lifetime employability.

The pursuit of lifetime employability and the pursuit of leadership may have different objectives, but behavior wise, they are one and the same. As you read, consider the two to be interchangeable.

Self-Governance

Embedded in the lessons and concepts of this book is the assumption that the reader, regardless of their status in the organization, maintains an acceptable regimen of self-governance . . . an ability to recognize changing trends and adjust accordingly. Critical in today's workplace is an ability to adapt to new concepts, new paradigms, and new expectations.

The laws of human nature, including the ability to influence others, are timeless. They remain the same as they have for centuries. The environment and circumstances in which those laws are applied, however, are changing at an ever-increasing pace. Having the ability to learn, unlearn and re-learn accordingly has never been more essential.

Quotients

Inside the four P's of *Principles, Performance, Perception and Politics,* are a collection of attributes and qualities that are the heart of this book. So, to present them, we had to consider how best to portray those attributes.

The common theme, or framework, we employed in our previous publication was a blueprint for leadership in the 21ˢᵗ century. If an architect's blueprint is the framework for constructing a building, we asked, what might the framework of the four P's, or lifetime employability look like? Our focus in the *'Me' Enterprise'* was on the *what's*. In this publication, our focus gets to the *how's*.

That brought us to the concept of quotients, which serve as a measure of how you rate in a given area. In this case, that is our method of measuring how principled you are as an individual; how well you perform your job; and how well you are perceived by your bosses and co-workers. Quotients became the yardstick for examining the qualities and attributes of the four P's.

Disclaimer: Keep in mind as you read, the four P's are not about the basic ABC's of doing your job. We leave those core skills, such as certifications or other pre-requisites, to your company. The four P's are about the skills that determine how well you do your jobs.

All accountants, for example, require a certification to become a CPA. But those who possess the additional soft skills of how to engage others, how to market themselves, how to politically maneuver in the workplace, etc., to complement their accountant certification, are the ones who separate themselves from the rest. They are the most sought after and the ones most assured of lifetime employability.

Those are the quotients we intend to address.

House of Lifetime Employability

Taking the theme of our last publication, *The Blueprint for the 'Me' Enterprise,* one step further, this book is put forth in a consistent realm, that of building a house . . . which we describe as a house of lifetime employability! What you look for in building or buying a house is the perspective from which we have organized this book.

At a minimum, you look for a solid foundation (your principles), a substantial structure of pillars (your performance), and a solid roof (how you are perceived and how you manage the power politics of your organization). Those are the same basic components which are essential to leadership and lifetime employability. As you navigate these pages, you will find the book organized accordingly:

- *Your Foundation* consists of the fundamental attributes needed to begin your competitive journey to sustained employment in the 21st Century. Your foundation is the set of principles and values that guide your behavior.

- *Your Supporting Pillars* are the qualities that are determine how well you perform your job; your ability to excel and navigate the complexities of todays' workplace. And,

- *Your Roof,* which you can think of as your personal brand. How you are perceived by your bosses and co-workers? How do you project yourself and how would you be described in the workplace? How do you navigate the politics of your organization?

As we examine the elements of the Four P's, think of each of them in terms of quotients, or how you would measure yourself in each of them. Further, view those quotients in the context of a structure. How solid are the principles that guide you, your foundation? How would you measure up in terms of your supporting pillars, your performance? And, what about the face you project to those around you, your roof?

To examine those Four P's, *Principles, Performance, Perception and Politics*, we will do so as a collection of quotients. Those quotients, in our collective view, represent your *House of Leadership,* or your *House of Lifetime Employability.*

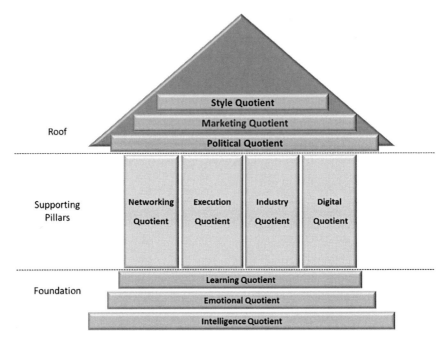

Life Time Employability Framework

To be more specific,

- *Your Foundation* begins with (1) your intelligence, your *IQ*; (2) followed by your ability to effectively engage and manage your emotions: your Emotional Quotient, or *EQ*; and, (3) your ability to learn or grasp new concepts: your Learning Quotient, or *LQ*.

- *Your Supporting Pillars* are, (4) your ability to attract others into your realm: your Networking Quotient, or *NQ;* (5) your ability to deliver results,: your Execution Quotient, or *XQ; (6)* your ability to discern the various industry segments: your Industry Quotient, or your *InQ*; and, (7) your technology savvy: your Digital Quotient, or *DQ*.

 and,

- *Your Roof* is how you project yourself to others, which consists of, (8) your ability to market or brand yourself, your Marketing Quotient or your *MQ*; (9) your ability to understand and engage the politics of your organization, your Political Quotient or your *PQ*; and, finally, (10) your personal style or the manner in which you engage others: your Style Quotient, or your *SQ*.

With that analogy, we provide a framework from which to understand, assess, and improve those elements we believe to be the foundation of sustained employability and leadership in the 21st century.

Curiosity

One final assumption we make in putting forward this thesis, is that of you having an active level of curiosity. Never before has the business world undergone so many changes so fast than in the past fifty years. Those changes will continue to be even more dramatic in the next fifty. Therefore, a high level of curiosity is an essential underpinning to navigating and incorporating those changes.

We assume you bring that curiosity into your work and into the reading of this book.

With those observations and assumptions serving as its premise, we offer you *The Keys to Lifetime Employability: Principles, Performance, Politics and Perception.*

Introduction

AARON MCKENZIE WAS at a crossroads. He was twenty-eight years old and possessed an MBA from a leading university where he graduated with honors. He had just received his second promotion into the management ranks of his company, a logistics firm in the Midwest, yet he felt uncertain about his new assignment and his career. Touted by his boss as an emerging, next generation leader less than three years out of graduate school, he wondered if he really had what it would take to succeed in his new role.

Instead of being excited about his promotion, he felt conflicted, not certain if he would enjoy the new managerial role, or, if he was even qualified for it. The logistics industry had changed drastically in the past decade and was still changing in this age of digitization and disruption.

Orders that once came from companies in New York, Chicago and San Francisco, are now coming from Shanghai, Hong Kong and Singapore. Interstate is now international. What once were forklift operators, are now computer operators. Because of new technologies, from receiving, to storing, to packing, to shipping, and distribution, what once took weeks, now takes a matter of days. The work, once requiring a crew of twelve, could now be performed by three individuals.

When he first joined his company, the average employee was white,

55+ years old, and possessed a high school diploma. They were baby boomers that had been with the company for years. In his new role, his workforce were under thirty, multi-racial, multi-cultural and most would have college degrees, if not graduate degrees. Multicultural GenX'rs and Millennials had a different attitude about their work than boomers. They had a different set of values.

The skills required of an employee today are dramatically different than twenty years ago. So are those of a manager. What once was a management philosophy of "command and control" is now one of "trust and track".

Though he had been with his company for less than three years, Aaron prided himself in being a quick learner. He knew the processes of the logistics business. He knew the technologies and had gained a reputation as an up-and-comer. Nonetheless, he was torn. This new position was taking him into a new realm of management. Instead of fourteen employees, he would now be responsible for fifty-five. Instead of being accountable for a single cost-center, he would now have the responsibility for the strategy and P&L financial performance of an entire Division. Additionally, he would inherit responsibility for managing the Six Sigma Quality program for the company, which would give him the added expectation of representing his company as a thought leader within his industry. His actions would be visible far beyond his team the higher-ups of his company. He would be interacting with his peers and leaders from an entire industry, both domestic and international.

If he were going to succeed in this new role, he had some growing to do, and some new skills to acquire. He had to expand the scope of his interests and capabilities far beyond what they are today. In short, he had to get into self-development mode quickly.

His company had drastically scaled back its training department during the financial downturn. The company offered a series of training programs, including a management training class, but it was limited to its company's processes, and very basic offerings and core skills, such as decision-making, prioritizing, and conflict management. Aaron knew he would need more than that. If he were going to get what he needed to be successful in his new role, that burden would be his, not the company's.

- *What more would he have to learn?*
- *Who would he be able to turn to for guidance?*
- *How would he stay abreast of the new technologies?*
- *How would he remain current or even relevant?*

For the first time since joining his company, Aaron felt that he was on his own. What in other times would be a cause for celebration, was a cause for concern and apprehension.

*   *   *

Welcome to the 21st century workplace. There are many Aaron McKenzie's in the workforce today, across all industries and professions. The number continues to increase. There is a growing gap between the emerging challenges of today's leaders, and the resources that companies provide its leaders to meet those challenges.

Regardless of your industry and regardless of the size and nature of your company, you are being impacted by the forces of technology, globalization and the disruptive nature characterized as the *Uberization* of companies and management. How you deal with those changes are up to you. There are many moving parts in the mosaic of lifetime employability. And as is our social and process engineering nature, we attempted to dissect and analyze them all.

We found the best analysis came in the form of the traits, characteristics and practices one must demonstrate if they are to achieve sustained employability in this age of digitization, globalization and disruption. In the early 20th century, employers looked at IQ as the measure of employability for prospective hires. Toward the end of the 20th century, EQ, or one's "emotional intelligence" had been added to the equation.

Those characteristics are still important, but as we forge headlong into a new millennium and a far more complex world, there are many more "Q"s' necessary to achieve and sustain success.

We don't profess to have captured them all, but from our collective vantage point, having seen the birth of the Internet and how it has transformed our world into a workplace of Nano-technologies and artificial intelligence, we do profess these to be essential.

Welcome to *The Four Keys to Lifetime Employability: Principles, Performance, Politics and Perception.*

PART I

Your Foundation

Every sustainable structure is founded on a solid foundation . . . one capable of sustaining the winds of a hurricane, the rains of a monsoon, and the ravages of fire. Your career should be no different.

The first of the Four "P"s is "Principles", those fundamental attributes required to even be a part of the conversation.

CHAPTER 1
IQ: Intelligence Quotient

Introduction

L ET'S FACE IT . . . YOU have to have some degree of intelligence to compete in today's marketplace. You don't have to be the smartest person in the room, but you do have to be smart enough to comprehend the nuances and complexities of your work environment. Technology alone can be mind-boggling. When you add in factors such as globalization and market disruption, it helps to be able to differentiate what is coming and what is going, both in your company and in the marketplace.

Hiring managers are not necessarily looking for *Summa* or *Magna Cum Lauds*. But they do look for those that can solve complex problems and formulate and execute competitive strategies in this ever increasing digital and complex environment.

It is for that reason that we begin with the oldest and most fundamental Q's . . . your IQ or intelligence quotient.

The words "intelligent" or "intelligence", and "IQ" are as common to us as are the words "smart", "genius" or "brilliant". They have been instilled in us since childhood to tell us that we are either "smart" or "not very smart". In school we took "IQ" exams to measure and prove just how smart we are. The words took on a social connotation, and in some instances, a social stigma. They could be an enabler or source of discouragement and demotivation. They could serve as a barrier or inhibitor to what we could or could not accomplish in life. Once the phrase, "he's not very smart" is bestowed upon someone, our expectations are automatically lowered for that individual, consciously or subconsciously. At one point in his life, Albert Einstein was deemed to be "not very smart" only to later be classified a genius (very smart).

The purpose of this chapter is to offer some perspective on those words and assumptions, especially in the context of the workplace and lifetime employability. We will begin with the basics . . . a brief look at the very origins of the words and how they evolved to establish the connotations and assumptions they did, and in some respects, proceed to demolish them. We will also look at some of the early studies about intelligence, and how our intelligence was viewed to be "fixed" and unable to be developed or improved. Then, we will examine how more recent studies offered a somewhat new and different perspective, and how our intelligence can indeed be developed.

Finally, we will attempt to put it all together as to how we can use and develop those key elements of our intelligence toward the objective of sustaining lifetime employability.

Let us start at the beginning . . .

Intelligence and IQ

The English word *intelligence* derives from the Latin nouns *intelligentia* or *intellēctus*, which in turn stem from the verb *intelligere*, meaning to comprehend or perceive. In the Middle Ages, *intellēctus* was the scholarly technical term for understanding, and a translation for the Greek philosophical term *nous*. Got all that?

Since those early beginnings, as the study of human behavior evolved, the term migrated from the realm of philosophy to become a central ingredient in psychology. Today, the study of intelligence has advanced significantly since those early origins, however psychologists are still debating its very definition.

Despite those differing views, scientists and behaviorists generally conclude its definition is:

The mental capability to, among other things, reason, plan, solve problems, think abstractly, comprehend complex ideas, learn quickly and learn from experience.

From Intelligence to IQ

The term intelligence quotient (IQ) emerged as the measure of intelligence in the early 1900's. The term "IQ" was coined by a psychologist named William Stern while at the University of Breslau in Germany in 1912. Though, there has been much refinement over the years, the IQ test remains the standard for measuring intelligence. The tests for IQ are designed not only to assess book learning, a narrow academic skill, or test-taking abilities, but to assess an individual's broader and deeper comprehension of his or her surroundings. Or, how well are they able to understand a situation and effectively solve problems?

From these standards, according to studies, it appears that roughly two-thirds of the population score between 85 and 115; a very minute percentage, about 2.5 percent of the population, scores above 130; and, a similar percentage scores 70.

While that is all a mildly interesting background, what we really want to know are:

- *Does intelligence take different forms, or different dimensions?*

- *Can I develop or enhance my intelligence or IQ? And if so, how;*

- *How does my IQ affect my performance at work?*

- *How does my IQ affect my reputation or brand?*

- *How can I best apply my IQ in different situations at work?*

- *And lastly, what do I need to take away from reading this chapter, as it relates to lifetime employability?*

Given the various dimensions of intelligence that have emerged in recent years, we propose to present this chapter in two parts: (1) the growing understanding of intelligence as a science and (2) how it affects us in the workplace. Ultimately, we intend to leave you with a fundamental understanding of the subject, and how intelligence is developed and applied toward the objective of achieving lifetime employability.

Let's go to work . . .

Our Growing Understanding of Intelligence

PART I: Types of Intelligence

To take the analysis of intelligence one step further, in the 1980's, another psychologist, Howard Gardener led a series of studies to examine other elements of our intellect. He studied things such as talents and special abilities, which were traditionally viewed only as ancillary traits to intelligence. He determined those traits were not ancillary at all but were different forms of intelligence.

Just because someone is not good at math, Gardener concluded, it does not mean they are not intelligent. Intelligence comes in different forms or specialties he said, and in 1983, he wrote of nine different types of intelligence.

1. **Naturalist Intelligence**—Naturalist intelligence describes the ability to discriminate among living things (plants, animals) as well as sensitivity to other features of the natural world (clouds, rock configurations).

2. **Musical Intelligence**—Musical intelligence is the capacity to discern pitch, rhythm, timbre, and tone. This intelligence enables us to recognize, create, reproduce, and reflect on music as demonstrated by composers, conductors, musicians, vocalist, and sensitive listeners.

3. **Logical-Mathematical Intelligence**—Logical-mathematical intelligence is the ability to calculate, quantify, consider propositions and hypotheses, and carry out complete mathematical operations. Young adults with lots of logical intelligence are interested in patterns, categories, and relationships. They are drawn to arithmetic problems, strategy games and experiments.

4. **Existential Intelligence**—Sensitivity and capacity to tackle deep questions about human existence such as the meaning of life, why we die, and how we got here.

5. **Interpersonal Intelligence**—Interpersonal intelligence is the ability to understand and interact effectively with others. It involves effective verbal and nonverbal communication, the ability to note distinctions among others, sensitivity to the moods and temperaments of others, and the ability to entertain multiple perspectives.

6. **Bodily-Kinesthetic Intelligence**—Bodily-kinesthetic intelligence is the capacity to manipulate objects and use a variety of physical skills. This intelligence also involves a sense of timing and the perfection of skills through mind–body union. Athletes, dancers, surgeons, and crafts people exhibit well-developed bodily-kinesthetic intelligence.

7. **Linguistic Intelligence**—Linguistic intelligence is the ability to think in words and to use language to express and appreciate complex meanings. Linguistic intelligence allows us to understand the order and meaning of words and to apply meta-linguistic skills to reflect on our use of language. Young adults with this kind of intelligence enjoy writing, reading, telling stories or doing crossword puzzles.

8. **Intrapersonal Intelligence**—Intrapersonal intelligence is the capacity to understand oneself and one's thoughts and feelings, and to use such knowledge in planning in engaging others. This is strongly affiliated with emotional intelligence (EQ), which we will address in the next chapter.

9. **Spatial Intelligence**—Spatial intelligence is the ability to think in three dimensions. Core capacities include mental imagery, spatial reasoning, image manipulation, graphic and artistic skills, and an active imagination. Sailors, pilots, sculptors, painters, and architects all exhibit spatial intelligence. Young adults with this kind of intelligence may be fascinated with mazes or jigsaw puzzles, or spend free time drawing or daydreaming.

The concept of intelligence is no longer binary, but now multi-dimensional. Consider how this added understanding of intelligence can assist in assessing one's natural proclivities, strengths and weaknesses, and with making career choices.

What we used to believe was singular and monolithic in nature, we now know to be a complex system of data points and interactions that collectively reveal much more than if we are simply smart or not smart.

That web of intellectual transactions can be viewed as a "value chain" of data and processes, as reflected below.

The "Intelligence" Value Chain

There was a time when intelligence was simply intelligence. You were smart, real smart, or not very smart. Since those times, however, scientists have made significant advances in connecting the dots of intelligence.

Its foundation, we are told, begins with "data" (1); followed by the ability to analyze, process, and convert that data into "information" (2); then, translate that information into "knowledge" (3); and finally, the ability to *apply* that knowledge (4).

Scientists go on to tell us that the ability to use sound judgment in how we apply that knowledge, is what we would describe as "wisdom". It is sort of like "the shin bones connected to the knee bone", etc. Just as is the human body, we learned the that brain and intelligence, rather than being singular in nature, is a system of component parts.

That is also accompanied by the discovery that there are various forms of intelligence.

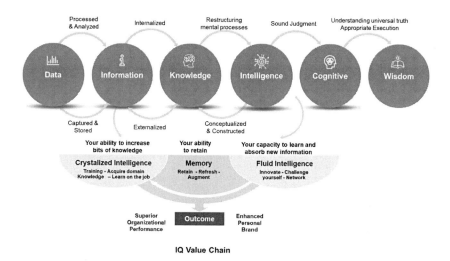

IQ Value Chain

As the chart reflects:

- *Data* is essentially the factual information that is available to us.

- *Information* is our ability to receive or absorb that data.

- *Analysis* is our ability to process and analyze that information to understand what it means.

- *Knowledge* is the analysis and conclusions we draw from that information as we perceive it.

- *Experience* is our ability to apply that knowledge in some useful way.

- *Cognition (our intuition, our gut feel)* can be thought of as inferences or new conclusions we draw from our knowledge or experiences.

- *Wisdom* can be viewed as the ability to consolidate those learnings in some new and creative way.

Fluid vs. Crystalized Intelligence

In the 1960's, a British psychologist named Raymond Cattell put forth the proposition that intelligence took two distinct forms. The first is our foundational intelligence. That, Cattell said, equates to our base level knowledge, generally formed through our early learnings and experiences. We learned 2 + 2 = 4. We learned our ABC's. We learned that dogs can bite and bees can sting. That foundational intelligence, which relies heavily on our experiences of past knowledge or learnings, is what Cattell referred to as "crystalized" intelligence.

He then introduced a second type of intelligence that equates to our ability to grasp new learnings or new experiences, which he referred to as "fluid" intelligence. That is the form of intelligence that makes us adept at grasping new experiences, new concepts, and solving new problems. Cattell, along with one of his former students, John Horn, went on to research the subject further and write a series of publications on fluid versus crystallized intelligence. It was their work which changed a number of those earlier beliefs on the subject.

Their work was also instrumental in destroying another earlier theory, that intelligence could not be developed. That belief was dramatically changed when they conducted a variety of studies which demonstrated that fluid intelligence could indeed be developed.

Those studies put the subject of intelligence in a brand-new light.

Add Memory into the Mix

On top of all the distinctions we have learned, between crystallized and fluid intelligence; the different dimensions of intelligence; and our levels of intelligence; there is yet another dimension to consider . . . our memories. Memory is defined as our ability to encode, store and retrieve information, and is obviously vital to drawing on our intelligence. Memory is essentially our ability to recall experiences and the retention of information over time.

For the purposes of this discussion, think of memory in three categories, as portrayed by the below graphic by Luke Mastin:

- *Our Sensory memory* is associated with our senses of touch, taste, smell, hearing, or seeing. Our sensory memory is fleeting and short lasting.

- *Our Short-term memory* is triggered by conversations or reading, etc. It is longer lasting, but again can be fleeting. How long do you remember a person's name when you are introduced?

- *Our Long-term Memory* is, as the term suggests, a memory that lasts a lifetime. An example would be remembering your street address or your phone number from childhood.

It is our long-term memory that is most essential to our lifetime employability. Its absence is what we refer to as *transactional* memory. You may be able to retain the transactions and conversations of the day, or even a week or month. But transactional memory does not equip you for the lifetime of new learnings you will have to retain, such as new procedures or new technologies associated with your work. So, the challenge is improving and developing our memories.

As the chart illustrates, long-term memory can be broken down into multiple, self-explanatory categories. Those categories collectively illustrate the many types of transactions we will have to remember to retain those new learnings.

How is your memory? Do you retain events only on a short-term or transactional basis? Or do you have long-term memory? There are a wide range of techniques and exercises to enhance your memory. To achieve lifetime employability, you will need to make yourself available to all that you reasonably can.

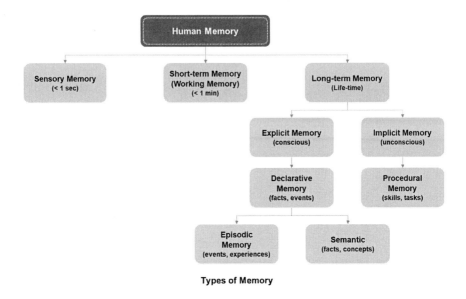

Types of Memory

A Meta-View of Intelligence

When you put all these dimensions together, it is clear that intelligence is not as straightforward and binary as behaviorists once believed. Considering all the dimensions and facets we just reviewed, if you put it all into the "Intelligence Value Chain" cited earlier, it might look something like this.

Part II—Intelligence in the Workplace

Intelligence is clearly a factor that impacts every aspect of our lives. That is especially true in the workplace. In this era of digitization and globalization, the demands of our work requiring us to know, understand, and recall new information has expanded exponentially. There was a time when we could work comfortably within a specific domain, such as assembly, or accounting, or computing. If we understood the processes associated with that activity, we could get by with that basic knowledge or intelligence. We may not have thrived in our industry, but at least we could survive.

Today, it is no longer sufficient to understand assembly, or manufacturing, or accounting, we must now understand the finances for the manufacturing sector, and the global environment in which it resides. Our need for intelligence and recall has extended beyond the basic processes of our jobs, to encompass the vertical sector in which our work resided.

Today, as technology has emerged to become a dominant player in terms of how our work is performed, our intelligence demands have increased yet again. We not only have to apply the intelligence related to performing our jobs, and knowledge of the industry sector of our jobs, to understand how technology executes the task related to our jobs. Digitization has introduced a whole new dimension to the workplace, and in doing so, placed a whole new dimension on our intelligence needs.

The sheer magnitude of the intelligence-related demands of our jobs can be overwhelming. And with leaders or aspiring leaders, those demands can be even more so.

To gain some sense of how to approach those growing demands, let's go back to the basics.

We examined the core building blocks of intelligence: data, information, analysis, knowledge, experience, intuition, and wisdom. We believe it is those same core building blocks that constitute the formula for lifetime employability.

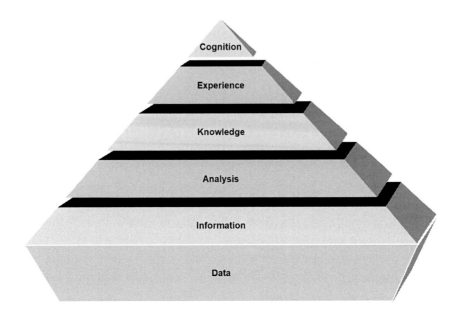

Intelligence Building Blocks for Lifetime Employability

So, how do those building blocks of intelligence apply to our day-to-day work? Fundamentally, as leaders or aspiring leaders, we can assume that our jobs contain three major buckets:

- *Strategy*—Planning and setting directions.
- *Governance*—Oversight or Controls, and
- *Operations*—The day-to-day execution of work.

And within each of those buckets are the same three dimensions that must be managed: people, processes, and technology. And specific to the issue of intelligence, each of those buckets can be divided into specific areas of responsibility. For example,

Strategy could require knowledge and intelligence associated with the activities of creating new ideas, commercializing those ideas into products, developing intellectual property, and the ability to articulate those new ideas into a vision.

Operations could require one to be knowledgeable of the portfolio of products, the profit and loss associated with that portfolio, knowing how to scale the portfolio, and knowing the industry.

Governance could include the need for knowledge or intelligence about company policy and laws, or even forensics.

It is conceivable that no matter the industry, and no matter the nature of our work, managers or aspiring managers can view their work in those three major buckets or dimensions and consider them to be timeless. So, lifetime employability means being "smart" or, at a minimum, knowledgeable within those domains. The smarter the better.

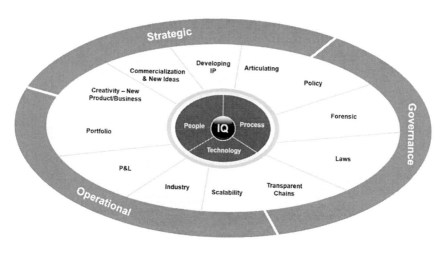

IQ at Workplace

Levels of Intelligence in the Workplace

So, within the context those three major activities and the competitive environment in which we work, how do we rate ourselves?

For starters, we can't be as generous in how we rate our intelligence in the workplace as we are about general subjects. We must have "domain knowledge" or "thought leadership" as it relates to our work. Being of only "average" intelligence regarding our jobs and our industry is a one-way ticket out.

We should assume that most everyone in the workplace are of average intelligence, even if you believe otherwise. Consider your colleagues to be reasonably smart, knowledgeable and able to conceptualize their basic work requirements. Then there are those who are more capable of understanding their work environment. Consider them "conceptual".

Then, there are the "super smart" that employ a combination of their intelligence with high levels of emotional intelligence. You typically find them in leadership positions and with active followers. Lastly, we have our geniuses. They combined their intelligence with their emotional intelligence, and their wisdom. They are many times described as the visionaries who formulate new ideas and concepts.

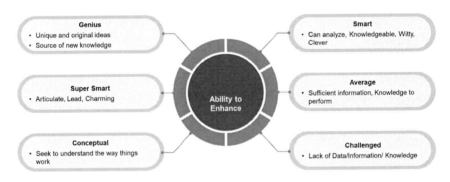

Level of Intelligence at Workplace

Developing Your IQ

Now, depending on how you rated yourself, the question we are left with is, "Can we do anything about it?" Can we actually develop or improve our intelligence?

In contrast to earlier beliefs by behavioral scientists that our intelligence is what it is, and we are stuck with it for a lifetime, later studies have proved otherwise. Experiments, such as those conducted by Cattell and Horn, have demonstrated that our intelligence can indeed, be improved upon. That is especially true as it relates to our fluid intelligence, that which is critical to new learnings, and especially critical to lifetime employability. Behavioral scientists readily admit there is much to be learned about the human brain and our intelligence. One thing they have learned, however, is that the same principle, "use it or lose it", applies to our brains just as it does to our bodies.

Cognitive scientist and behavior therapist, Andrea Kuszewski says, "we can increase our fluid intelligence in a variety of ways." She offers the following techniques, as examples:

- *Try new things*—New activities, she says, trigger new areas of the brain. Variety she says, is the spice of life.

- *Push your limits*—Just as in strength building for your body, expanding your horizons mentally is a healthy way to develop your intelligence.

- *Use your whole brain*—Again, variety is key. From painting to learning a new language, to solving complex riddles or math problems, the therapist says challenge every aspect of your thought process.

- *Be Social*—Engaging other people, both in the work environment and socially stimulates brain activity in a variety of ways.

- *Stay Active*—Physical activity has a correlating benefit to stimulating brain activity and developing your intelligence.

Developing Your Intelligence in the Workplace—Your Investment in Yourself

In our previous book, *Emergence of the 'Me' Enterprise*, we spent a great deal of time discussing the need for individuals to invest in themselves much the way corporations invest in creating new products and services. Just as companies devote two, three, or four percent or more of their revenues to research and development, or R&D, those who thrive and survive in today's workplace apply the same concept to themselves.

Your investment in yourself is the way you develop your intelligence, continue learning new concepts, technologies and skills, and assure your lifetime employability. In previous decades, employee training and development was largely the burden of the employer and took place in the form of formal training workshops, conferences, or certification programs.

Today, in the era of the 'Me' Enterprise, the burden of development has largely shifted to the individual employee. Formal employee training programs sponsored by corporations was one of the many costs that were victimized during the economic downturn of the early 2000's. Corporate sponsored training programs have been largely reduced to the basics of performing your current job, and little if any, to preparing you for the future. On that, you are on your own.

As a baseline, given the many dimensions and nuances of intelligence, where are you strongest? Where are your weaknesses? How do you begin to improve your working intelligence?

Dimensions	Sensory Memory	Short Term Memory	Long Term Memory			
	Organized		Fluid			
	Current Job	Adjacent Markets	New Markets			
	Operations	Governance	Strategy			
	People . Process . Technology					
IQ Types	**IQ Level**					
	Genius	Super Smart	Conceptual	Smart	Average	Challenged
Intrapersonal						
Spatial			?			
Interpersonal						
Naturalist						
Musical					?	
Logical - Math		?				
Existential						
Kinergetic						
Linguistic				?		

IQ : How am I doing?

The good news is there are more ways to invest in your own development. In addition to formal training programs, there are multiple distance learning and online course options, such as webinars, blogs, Ted Talks, and YouTube training.

In business, there is a painful history of successful companies who fell in love with their success. From the original PC makers who believed their products would last forever, to the Polaroid or Kodak companies, who believed digital film could never supplant their dominance, to Blockbuster Video, the list is endless. The axiom is clear . . . success can breed complacency, and complacency breeds obsolescence.

We are no different. Companies have Research and Development Departments whose purpose is to look forward and develop new products or technologies to maintain their relevance and dominance. We have ourselves. Through whatever means necessary, your investment in yourself is your R&D.

Invest heavily and wisely.

Health / Fitness / Work life Balance				
	Formal Training	Relationship Learning	Learn/Understand/Teach/ Inspect (LUTI)	Customer Focus
Crystalized Intelligence	Strengthen Foundation	Guidance / Feedback	Relevant	Sustain
Fluid Intelligence	Learning New Capabilities	New Horizons / New Tips	Lead	Thrive
CI + FI + Articulation = Wisdom				
Wisdom	Consciousness / Value	Visibility	Inspire	Create New Opportunities

Investment Framework for IQ at Workplace

* * *

Richard Dawson was up for promotional consideration for the third time in twelve months. Twice within the past year, he had applied for a leadership role in the Technical Division. And twice, he was turned down. Richard was an excellent troubleshooter and problem solver when it came to technology. His logic was flawless and his ability to conceptualize technical solutions surpassed everyone in his group.

When it came to solving problems, Richard was many times considered the "smartest person in the room". Yet, he failed to impress when it came time to select group leaders.

The feedback he received on both previous occasions was the same:

"Though highly competent as a technologist, Richard needs to develop his leadership and interpersonal skills to be given serious consideration to lead in this Division."

But, as the saying goes, "third time's the charm."

On this occasion, Richard came into the interview prepared. He had a one-page outline, listing his accomplishments and the array of courses and workshops he had attended in the past six months, including "Toastmasters" and the Dale Carnegie course on "How to Win Friends and Influence People." He began his interview by saying, "I know in the past I have not been regarded as a strong leadership candidate in this organization. You have given me the feedback to prove it. But, I also have this list of actions I've taken to address those deficits; and I think I'm ready. I know I have to earn your confidence to be considered for this position, and that is exactly what I intend to do."

Richard invested in himself. He got his promotion.

* * *

Your Intelligence Quotient or IQ is not the single or even foremost measure employers look for when making hiring or promotion decisions. But it is a critical dimension in those decisions . . .

- *Your ability to solve problems*
- *Your vertical knowledge*
- *Your technical knowledge*
- *Your ability to grasp new concepts, new ideas*

Combined with your EQ, your ability to "win friends and influence people", those are the elements employers will always look for regarding your intelligence. To maintain your readiness, remember the following:

Crystallized + *Fluid* + *Memory* = **Lifetime Employability**

Are you ready? How would you rate yourself, given all the dimensions we've discussed?

Guiding Principles

1. Complement your intelligence with AI and other technology tools.

2. Remember current jobs will be replaced with "repetitive intelligence" technology—keep moving up the value. Disrupt yourself. analog/digital (answering machine).

3. Listening, Understanding, Teaching and Inspecting is the best way to enhance intelligence (LUTI).

4. Invest in learning that requires testing, certifying and presenting (stretch; Test yourself). Seek CII (Continuous Innovation and Improvement).

5. Select institutions for formal training that offers scenario planning, case studies and discussions.

6. (More "traditional" learning; 2-way learning) Go beyond online learning from Khan Academy.

7. Do not be intimidated to network with higher intelligence individuals and groups.

8. Suspend judgement of others—Compliment other's intelligence. Leverage other's value. Be aware of other's hidden intelligence.

9. Leverage others—you cannot know *everything!*

10. Calibrate your IQ when looking for new opportunities. Think through the skills you have vs. what the skills the opportunity requires. Do your homework.

CHAPTER 2
EQ: Emotional Quotient

Of all the skills and attributes of leadership, none is as essential as Emotional intelligence.

—Travis Bradberry

Introduction

IF YOUR INTELLIGENCE is your ability to process and act on information, your *emotional intelligence* is your ability to process and act on information in terms of how you engage others. Emotional Intelligence (EI) has emerged to become one of the most important characteristics of effective leadership. Your Emotional Quotient (EQ) is the measure of EI, just as your IQ is a measure of your intelligence.

Compared to intelligence and IQ, the concept of emotional intelligence is a relatively new concept. The very discovery of emotional intelligence and the notion that one's emotional intelligence, or EI, was essential to leadership, was not put forth until the middle of the 20th century. Though the construct of EI or EQ (the terms or used interchangeably) has lagged behind IQ in terms of its history, it has quickly emerged to become one of the most critical success factors in the world of business. In fact, there are scientist and business leaders that have deemed EQ to be *the* most critical factor.

While we do not engage in that particular debate, we do agree that emotional intelligence or EQ, is essential to one's lifetime employability, and view it to be part of that critical foundation. Let's explore why.

In this chapter, we will examine:

- *The basic elements that comprise Emotional Intelligence and your Emotional Quotient (EQ)*
- *How EI affects a leader's performance*
- *How EI affects a leader's brand*
- *How EI is used with different audiences and circumstances*
- *How to strengthen your EQ*
- *Current Environment/Guiding Principles*

Again, let's start at the beginning . . .

Emotions

Our emotions, or how we feel, affect our thoughts, actions and our lives. They not only define what and how we feel; they influence every action we take, and the enthusiasm, or lack thereof, in which we take them. They can be both positive and negative and can be expressed both verbally and non-verbally. It has long been believed that the human experience contained six basic emotions: happiness, sadness, anger, surprise, fear and disgust. A recent study by the National Institute of Science, however, concluded there were as many as twenty-seven emotions that we commonly exhibit:

27 Commonly Exhibited Emotions		
Admiration	Confusion	Interest
Adoration	Craving	Joy
Aesthetic Appreciation	Disgust	Nostalgia
Amusement	Empathetic pain	Romance
Anxiety	Entrancement	Sadness
Awe	Envy	Satisfaction
Awkwardness	Excitement	Sexual Desire
Boredom	Fear	Sympathy
Calmness	Horror	Triumph

Twenty Seven Commonly Exhibited Emotions

Another behaviorist used the following graph to depict our world of emotions and the reactions that tend to follow:

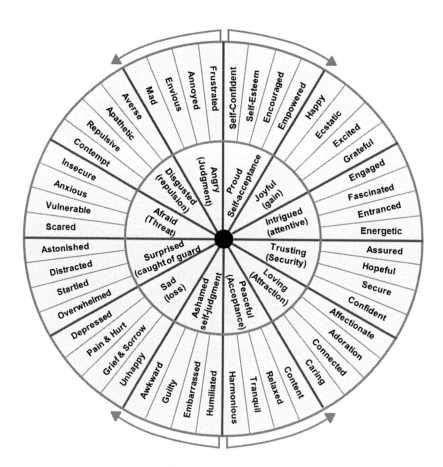

Feelings Wheel

Emotional Intelligence

Emotional intelligence (EI) is about being in tune with our own and other's emotions; and our ability to effectively factor those emotions into the way we interact with others. For example, if you are having a rotten day and you express that in the way you are speaking and behaving, if I ignore that in the way we are engaging one another, I'm not displaying emotional intelligence. EI is about being aware of emotions and acting on them.

Different behavioral scientists have defined EI and EQ in varying terms, but tend to agree on this basic definition:

Emotional Quotient defined:

EQ is the measure of an individual's ability to recognize their own emotions as well as those of others; to discern between different feelings and label them appropriately; and to use that emotional information to guide their thinking and behavior.

For us lay people, that simply means, (1) can we detect when we're feeling our own emotions; (2) can we detect other's emotions and (3) can we use that information to guide us to do the right thing? That, behaviorists tell us, is essential in our ability to lead.

The Origins of EI and EQ

The term emotional intelligence first appeared in a paper published by Michael Beldoch in 1964, and ever since, has been the subject of much analysis and scrutiny by both behavioral scientists and practitioners. Despite its emergence, EI was not recognized as a critical ingredient of effective leadership until 1995 when science journalist and author, Daniel Goleman published his findings in a book he titled, appropriately enough, *Emotional Intelligence*. Since that time, other behavioral scientists have come forward to offer other various insights on the subject, but Goleman's basic premise that EI is critical to leadership has remained.

Following Goleman's groundbreaking study on the subject of EI, there have been other behaviorists who have been recognized for advancing EI's significance in leadership. In 2004, Peter Salovey and John Mayer, also behavioral scientists and authors, conducted a series of studies which concluded that EI was essential in an individual's ability to process emotional information and use it to navigate their day-to-day environment. Other behavioral scientists have studied the subject and offered subtle variations on its minor details, but all agreed on one significant conclusion . . . people who demonstrate high levels of emotional intelligence have greater mental health, improved job performance, and superior leadership skills.

Through the 1990's and into the 2000's, behavioral scientists, business leaders and practitioners have raised the significance of EI to a new level. Emotional intelligence, practitioners conclude, is one of the top two or three most essential attributes of an effective leader.

How We Express Emotions

We express our emotions, and acknowledge those of others, both verbally and non-verbally. What we say and how we say it, as well as our facial expression, our eye contact, how we sit and how we stand, all convey emotions. That communication is also tilted toward "sending" rather than "receiving". As leaders, we are conditioned to tell others what to do and how to do it. Unfortunately, we are far less conditioned to listen to those we lead. How do they respond, verbally or nonverbally, when being told what to do? How enthusiastically or un-enthusiastically will they execute those commands? It is our emotional intelligence, or lack of, that gives us the answer to those questions.

Further, it is our emotional intelligence that helps us differentiate how we respond in different situations, different settings or with different groups. Did you ever have a boss or colleague try to conduct serious business at a social gathering, while everyone else is engaged in small talk? Or, have you listened to someone from one country speak to an individual from another country, without considering the cultural or language differences that may exist between the two? That is emotional intelligence, or in some cases, the lack thereof.

Developing Your EI

Are you comfortable with verbally expressing your emotions? Are you comfortable with acknowledging the emotions of others? Are you a "listener", or are you more of a "teller"? Do you "transmit" and "receive" in your conversations with others? Or are you primarily a "sender"? Do you tend to factor emotions into your interactions, or do you take a "just the facts" approach?

However you choose to rate yourself, the good news is your emotional intelligence can be developed and improved upon. Behaviorists have characterized EI as a skill which, through conditioning and training, can be learned and incorporated into your natural interactions.

For many years, emotional intelligence was thought to be a natural trait. Practitioners and behavioral scientists alike had the attitude that *you either have it or you don't... You're either born with it or not.* However, since those early theories, many scientific studies and corporate training and coaching programs have proven otherwise. In a recent article, published in the Harvard Business Review, author and scientist Tomas Chamorro-Premuzic, the Chief Talent Scientist at ManpowerGroup and a professor of business psychology, best summarized the debate when he wrote:

"Our levels of EQ may be firm, but not rigid. While our ability to identify and manage our own and others' emotions is fairly stable over time, influenced by early childhood experiences and even genetics, that does not mean we cannot change it. And many companies are demonstrating that."

Chamorro-Premuzik, who also serves as an associate at Harvard's Entrepreneurial Finance Lab, further states, "good coaching programs do work!"

Corporate leadership programs and private institutions alike are putting more and more emphasis on the subject of emotional intelligence. In addition to sales, marketing, profit and loss, leaders are learning how to listen, ask questions, and demonstrate empathy.

Travis Bradberry is another expert on the topic of EI. His firm, TalentSmart, and other firms like his have made a career out of assessing and developing the emotional intelligence of the executives of Fortune 500 companies. Training and development companies, as well as behavioral scientists, professional coaches and executive search firms, all incorporate the development of EQ into their services. They have discovered the significance of EQ as a critical leadership skill and treat the development of that skill as they would with any other skill. From learning to play the piano, to hitting a golf ball, emotional intelligence is a learned behavior.

Through assessments, instruction and reinforcement, executives and leaders are improving their EI behaviors, and hence their leadership capabilities, by developing seemingly mundane activities, such as:

- *Body posture*
- *Eye contact*
- *Asking questions*
- *Listening*
- *Paraphrasing*
- *Self-disclosure*

Bradberry, who also authored the book, *Emotional Intelligence 2.0*, points out a significant distinction between your EQ and IQ. "Whereas your IQ basically remains the same as you age, your EQ can grow and be developed." Bradberry goes on to state:

"There is no known connection between IQ and emotional intelligence; you simply cannot predict emotional intelligence based on how smart someone is. Intelligence is your ability to learn, and it's the same at age 15 as it is at age 50. Emotional intelligence, on the other hand, is a flexible set of skills that can be acquired and improved with practice."

EI in the Workplace

"While emotional intelligence may be rarer than book smarts, my experience says it is actually more important in the making of a leader. You just can't ignore it.

Jack Welch Retired CEO of GE

The workplace is, at one level, a somewhat simpler environment when it comes to EI; but at another level, it becomes far more complicated as you are confronted with different situations. When we perform well and get positive feedback for that performance, we think positive thoughts and, by extension, we exude positive feelings. By contrast, if we perform poorly or receive negative feedback, we think negatively, and therefore tend to respond negatively to others. Your employees and colleagues are no different. As the graphic below illustrates, reading your own or the emotions of others, can begin as a binary choice . . . positive or negative, black or white.

Different situations begin to add complexity to the challenges of EI, as we will discuss later, but the first question, for yourself or others, is "am I feeling positive, lively and in control? Or, do I feel the opposite . . . negative, agitated and out of control?"

How you answer and respond to that basic question has an effect on your work performance, and our "brand".

Where would you position yourself on the graph below? Where would others place you? If you're not on the right-hand side, you have work to do.

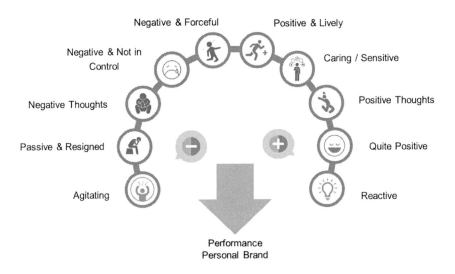

Channeling Feelings (Emotions in the Workplace)

*   *   *

Morten Gunderson worked for a European-based company that developed technology for the aerospace industry. He headed the development team that worked on new applications to improved communication links between satellites and space stations. His team was very proud of their work and the mission of their company. They were nearing completion of a prototype which, if successful, would mean millions of dollars in new orders for their company. It was also thought to serve as the catalyst to take their company public. They were reminded daily of those implications of their work.

On Friday, the group received an email notifying them of a meeting to be held at 10:00 AM the following Monday morning, where they would receive a major announcement.

The buzz about the pending meeting began immediately.

The prevailing thought was that the meeting would be to announce the details of the pending prototype demonstration, including who would be presenting, who would be in attendance, and where the presentation would take place. Both European and American companies had been following their progress closely and were expected to send representatives to the demonstration. Companies, ranging from Lockheed-Martin, to Tesla, to Airbus and Rolls Royce Aerospace were all expected to be in attendance. The stakes were high. Morten's boss, the head of the company's Aerospace Division yet four years younger than Morten, would lead the Monday morning meeting.

The Friday afternoon notification about the meeting gave the team members all weekend to speculate about its purpose. Many of the members hastily made arrangements to get together over the weekend to discuss anticipated roles for the upcoming prototype presentation, and where the presentation might take place. Rumors were already circulating that the prototype would be unveiled in Washington D.C., given the strong interest of American companies. By Monday morning, the rumors were rampant. By 9:45 AM, the team members had settled into their auditorium seats in preparation for the 10 AM announcement. They didn't have to wait long.

At two minutes past the ten o'clock hour, Morten's boss, referred to by team members as the "MBA Whiz Kid", arrived in the auditorium and wasted little time getting to the topic. The young Division VP had a reputation as having brains but no personality, and his presentation tended to reinforce that belief. He made no eye contact with his audience and kept his head down as he read from his notes.

Ladies and Gentlemen, the prototype presentation has been postponed. While I salute you for the tireless effort you have put into this project, circumstances have arisen, which I cannot go into at this time, that make it necessary for us to re-examine our strategy and our timeframe. I hope to have more information for you, perhaps as early as the end of this week.

*You all know the importance of what you are doing, and I believe that effort will pay even greater dividends than we had originally anticipated. The presentation **will** occur (he stated with emphasis), just perhaps not as we had originally planned! Please continue your work, and we hope to have further information for you shortly.*

Thank you.

With that terse announcement, which took less than a minute, Morten's boss exited the auditorium without discussion or entertaining questions. There was a palpable silence in the room, but the group's body language was equally palpable. Morten and his team members were left surprised, dumbfounded, and confused; and whatever explanation was to be given to the team would have to be provided by Morten, who had not even been briefed on the situation. He was now left to deal with his own conflicting emotions, as well as those of his team members.

The surprise announcement was like a giant ball being dropped into their laps with a thud. Morten was clearly agitated, but as the group's leader, it was his job to keep his staff motivated and focused. How motivated and focused could they be after hearing what they just heard?

Morten had a flood of emotions and he knew he must be able to quickly assess and determine his own emotions before he could help his team with theirs . . . like the announcement you get on an airline, "Before helping others, put your own gas mask on first." He was certainly surprised by the news and probably disappointed as well, but what else?

He was frustrated that the work he and his team had prepared to present was being postponed. And, he didn't even know the reason why it was postponed. Was it politics? Was it corporate posturing of some sort? What was it? He was angry that, with no knowledge of the situation, he would be left to deal with his team, on his own. What were his emotions? He would have to figure that out quickly if he were going to be able to effectively deal with the myriad of emotions his team members were probably feeling.

*   *   *

This scenario is a vivid example of why emotional intelligence (EI) is regarded as an essential attribute for effective leadership. In a span of less than two minutes, the productivity of Morten and his team was brought to a screeching halt. Their productivity and commitment were completely undermined by the seemingly unconscious actions of a senior leader who appeared to have no appreciation or awareness for how he approached this pivotal moment. The team was left frustrated, disappointed and unmotivated. Unless dealt with effectively and swiftly, the many emotions they were feeling could sidetrack months of work.

Situational Awareness

In addition to reading an individual's emotions, there is a second dimension which is equally critical to EI. That is "situational awareness". Who you respond to and how you respond depends on the place and the circumstance. Are you in a setting with just you and another individual? Are you in a group setting? Or, are you outside the workplace altogether, in a social setting for example?

Morten had twenty-three team members, ranging in ages from twenty-two to fifty, from four different countries and four different cultures. Would a large group meeting be appropriate? Or should he break them into small groups . . . or even 1x1? He decided to begin with the large group meeting, to be followed by smaller group meetings and individual discussions.

Your responses are somewhat different, depending on your setting. Being 1x1 with an individual, you can give your full attention to that individual. In a group setting, you have to "generalize" and sense the overall mood or emotions of the group as a whole. A social setting out of the office, in contrast, is not the place to delve too heavily in work related discussions, saving those for the workplace. Situational awareness, combined with emotional awareness, are the fundamental building blocks of EI.

As the below graph illustrates, there are multiple settings and situations of which you should be mindful. Social situations call for a very different approach to engaging others than you would in the workplace. As does how you interact in an individual setting versus a group setting.

Potential Situations

How you respond is dependent on the circumstances and where you respond. Test your responses based on the following two-minute self-assessment. As a starting point, the results can provide a gauge of your situational awareness and EI.

	1 & 1	1 & Many	1 & Social
What I see	Self Aware	Self Manage	Prepare
	Sense	Acknowledge	Seek Advice
	Recognize	Construct	Role Play
	Respond	Channel	Follow Up
	Cognizant	Relate	Recognize
What I do	Self Aware	Acknowledge	Prepare
	Sense /Tune	Calibrate	Advice
	Impact	Reaction	Role Play
	Dynamics	Network	Follow Up
	Q & A's	Success Factors	Stand Out
What I need to do	Self Aware	Observe	Decide
	Environment/Topic	Participate	Appropriateness
	Dynamics	Vulnerable	Be aware of Controversies
	Link	Involve	Tactful
	Connect	Network	Sensitive

Two Minute Assessment

The Impact of EI on Your Performance

The study of EI and EQ has revealed a fundamental premise that all of our actions and decisions are influenced in part, by our emotions. If we are passionate about our work, we are more engaged and enthused than if we were less passionate. If we are angry with our boss, or do not hold him or her in high regard, our actions tend to reflect those feelings. If my co-worker is from a different country or a different culture than my own, and I have predisposed views about that country, my attitudes and hence my actions toward that co-worker are likely to be reflected in those views.

In this age of globalization, digitization and disruption, our world of work has been turned upside down.

- *Our workforce is more diverse, in terms of race, age and gender.*
- *We work for and with individuals who are younger and have different experiences, and look different than ourselves.*
- *We view our approach to work differently, depending on our age group (i.e., baby boomers v. millennials).*

Further, our performance can differ when we're having a good day versus when things are going south. Those who tend to exhibit the highest levels of EI are measured more positively and more constructively in group situations than those who rank lower on the EI scale.

In many respects, our workplace has become a melting pot of races, genders, values, norms and religions. When we allow our feelings or predisposed views of those differences into our work environment, our performance tends to suffer, as does our ability to lead.

In 2000, John Antioco, CEO of Blockbuster Video, was approached by the founder of a small start-up online video company about a possible acquisition. Antioch considered online video to be a very small niche business and was offended that the founder of the small company had the audacity to ask fifty million for his fledgling enterprise that was not even profitable. Feeling insulted, Antioco angrily dismissed his suitor, ignoring the advice of many members of his leadership team.

That suitor was Reed Hastings, and his fledgling enterprise was called Netflix.

Today, Netflix has a roughly four billion market evaluation, while Blockbuster resides in the dustbin of companies that missed the mark. While analysts claim it was Antioco's lack of vision that affected his decision, those closest to the Blockbuster CEO attribute the missed opportunity to his inability to look beyond his own emotions and biases.

The marketplace is littered with examples of leaders being unable to look beyond the forest that is their own emotions to see the vision and overcome differences in the workplace. In most of those situations, it was the lack of emotional intelligence and not vision that was the preeminent factor in making poor business decisions.

Whether in an individual or group setting, our performance is reflected by our ability to factor the emotions of the situation into the decision-making process.

The Impact of EQ on Your "Brand"

Our emotional intelligence not only plays a major role in our leadership effectiveness and decision-making, it plays an equally critical role in how we are viewed by others.

In addition to the previously mentioned differences in our workplace, we also work in a more virtual and transient workplace. It is possible to have co-workers, even bosses we have never met face-to-face, working with us or directing us. Be they multi-national or work-at-home team members, they are rarely if ever seen. Fortunately, or unfortunately, they are judged not by what they do, but the impression we form of them from afar. Seemingly insignificant "sound bites" can define a co-worker or leader, serving as the basis for how we assess and view them.

When BP, the British oil conglomerate, suffered a massive oil spill in the Gulf of Mexico in 2010, CEO Tony Hayward left his home in England to be onsite in the Gulf, where he remained during the clean-up of the disaster. In an interview with a local TV station, he was asked to describe his feelings about the disaster. He responded, "I'm frustrated. I haven't slept in my own bed or seen my family in weeks. I want my life back."

Tony Hayward had the managerial skills to rise through the ranks of BP to become the CEO of the massive company. But his inability to look beyond the inconvenience of his own situation changed his life. Beyond the personal disruption he was experiencing, there were many Gulf Coast residents and businesses that were devastated by the disaster, in far greater terms. In that one moment, his failure to express empathy for those individuals defined him, both in the eyes of the public and the eyes of his company.

Within months, he was terminated, not for the work he had performed, but for how he was perceived. His personal brand, from that moment, was forever defined as one of being selfish, uncaring, and hence, unable to lead.

Contrast that situation to Starbucks CEO Kevin Johnson. The manager of a Starbucks store in Philadelphia had two black patrons arrested for no apparent reason, out of fear that they may create trouble. The men were professional real estate agents and had shown no signs of disruption. The incident escalated quickly and turned into a major boycott of Starbucks locations nationwide. Less than a week after the incident, Johnson was in Philadelphia to take action.

He dismissed the store manager and personally apologized to the two victims. Further, he announced that all stores, nationwide, would be closed on a day, for all Starbucks employees to undergo race and sensitivity training. Johnson was sensitive enough to understand the situation, and decisive enough to move quickly to get ahead of any potential blowback to the Starbucks brand.

What about Morten's boss? How was his brand affected by his behavior? As the leader of the Division, did he gain any "followers" by his lack of engagement? In negative situations or positive; when we get what we want or do not, our emotional intelligence invariably impacts our performance, and our reputation, or "brand".

Look at the below graphic and see if you react differently when you get what you want, as opposed to those occasions when you do not.

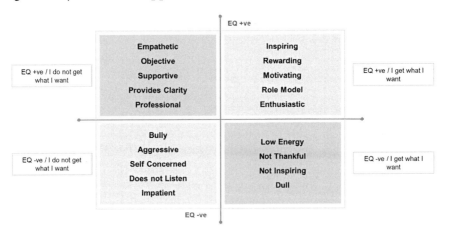

Impacts on Personal Brand

When You Have to Respond Up

Of the various scenarios in the workplace that require sensitivity and emotional intelligence, the one question that we hear the most is, "What do you do when you have a situation in which you have to confront your boss?" How do you raise a delicate or sensitive issue with the very person that can impact your livelihood? Consider Morten's situation.

*   *   *

Morten was disappointed for his team who had worked tirelessly for over nine months for this moment. But he was also frustrated with his boss, who appeared to show no sensitivity or awareness of how his announcement would affect his team. Further, he was given no advanced notice of the announcement, or any guidance as to how to manage the situation. He knew he wanted to express his frustration to his team, but he would need to do so in a way that would not undercut his boss or the company. Should he express his feelings to his boss as well?

Morten was angry and frustrated and had a lot he wanted to say. But should he express his feelings to his team, or even to his boss? Or was this a time to just listen to others and let them vent and express their emotions?

He needed time to think. But he knew he had to provide some immediate guidance to his team before they left the auditorium. As his team gathered their belongings in preparation to head for the exits, Morten came to a decision.

"Can everyone remain for a few minutes? I have something I'd like to say."

As the team members returned back to their seats, a quiet hush overcame the auditorium. Morten broke the silence.

"Folks, I am as surprised as you probably are at what just happened. In fact, I'm more than surprised. But I'll save that for later. Right now, I want to give you all a chance to digest what you just heard,

and the implications about what it means for how we continue with our work. And remember, we DO have work to complete.

While you reflect, I'll see what I can find out about the postponement, and how we proceed from here. Let's plan to meet tomorrow morning and I'll bring you up to date on what I found out. Meantime, please stay focused. We have a very important presentation to make.

Thanks folks. See you tomorrow morning."

*   *   *

Morten did not want his group to disperse feeling frustrated, confused or disappointed. Fortunately, he had the emotional intelligence to sense his own and team's feelings, and the situation. But he also knew that would not be sufficient. He had a delicate situation to confront with his boss.

*   *   *

After everyone had left the auditorium, Morten had the room to himself and had a chance to reflect on his own thoughts and feelings. He also had to decide what he should do next. He felt disappointment and frustration, both for himself and for his team. He decided he needed to express those feelings to his team members, but also to his boss.

In the brief moments of his solitude, he formulated a three-step plan of action. First, he would meet with his boss to express his own feelings and get his boss' input and guidance as to what to share with his team. Second, he would meet with his team as a group tomorrow morning to update them, based on his boss' guidance. Third, he would meet with his team members individually to allow them the opportunity to ask questions, or just to vent.

He planned to communicate his feelings to his boss and to his team members, but he knew he would have to treat each situation differently. His team members were of different ages, different countries, and different cultures. Four of them were virtual teammates, working remotely from their home office. They would possibly have a very different view of the situation than the other team members.

As he began to gather his belongings and head to his boss' office, he remembered a three-step communications formula he had learned in an "assertiveness training" class he had taken years ago. It was a formula for how to show empathy, yet effectively express yourself in conflicts or difficult situations. The formula, he was told applied to communicating with to your boss, subordinates or others. The steps were:

1. *Express Empathy*—"I realize you are in a difficult position . . . "
2. *State the conflict*—"However, I . . . "
3. *Suggest a Proposed Action or Next Step*—"Therefore, I propose that we . . . "

As he continued toward his boss' office, with that formula in mind, he envisioned a conversation with his boss that he hoped would go something like:

"I realize the situation you're dealing with is somewhat sensitive, and more complicated than you could express to the team **(Empathy)***, however, we now have a team that is very confused, disappointed and frustrated.* **(Conflict)** *Therefore, I would ask that you give me some guidance as to what I can communicate to the team, tomorrow morning."* **(Proposed action)***.*

Surprisingly, Morten's conversation with his boss went very well. His boss was appreciative of Morten's sensitivity to the situation, and he shared the reason for the postponement of the presentation. "I could not share this in an open forum", his boss told Morten, "but we have a potential merging of proposals with another player. I cannot share anything further at this time, but please let your team know, this could be very good for us."

The two then organized the messaging that Morten would be able to share with his team the following morning. Morten felt much better. He had new information that he thought would be received positively by the team, and he had experienced a good, open conversation with his boss.

*   *   *

How to Begin

Ben Cannon was the CEO of a mid-sized California-based technology company, specializing in the creation of custom simulations for companies wishing to creatively display their products and services. Every customer had a unique product and every order was a custom design, requiring close cooperation and collaboration across the company's divisions. The management team ranged from graphic designers to logistics managers, to marketing specialists. Close collaboration was a must.

Ben was known for offering unique and creative ways to communicate his message, and his Monday morning staff meetings were the perfect venue. As his team took their seat at the conference table on one such occasion, a round pinwheel-like card was in placed in front of each of them.

"You see this chart?" (the same chart illustrated at the beginning of this chapter) Ben began. "It is a summary of the emotions we experience every day. And those emotions factor into every conversation we have, with colleagues, subordinates, customers or partners, and more importantly, they factor into our decision making. Every decision our customers make is impacted by their emotions, and it's your job to be in tune with those emotions.

That begins with each of us being in touch with our own emotions, and then being able to detect the emotions of the person we are interacting with. Sometimes, they tell us their emotions verbally. And sometimes, we have to figure it out by their facial expression or their body language. Learn to be in tune with your own emotions; and the emotions of those with whom you communicate . . . be they employee, customer or partner.

I want to hear two statements in the way we communicate with each other . . .

'I feel (emotion)'

or,

'You seem (emotion)'

As simple as it sounds, you'll be amazed at how those simple statements, using this chart, will help us communicate better, lead better, and win more business."

Those simple words, "I feel" or "You seem" are the starting point for increasing your emotional intelligence. They get you in the habit of being more aware of individuals' emotions; and they verbally acknowledge the feelings of those around you.

Consider the following as the remaining key components from which to further develop your EI.

Steps to Putting Your EI into Action

Engagement framework for EQ

Step 1—Know Your Own Emotions

Step #1 in the EI continuum, according to behavioral scientists, is to know your own emotions and have the ability to properly deal with those emotions. Before Morten could effectively deal with his team or his boss, who happened to be four years younger, he had to come to grips with his own emotions. If you were in Morten's shoes, what would you be feeling? After your boss had shown virtually no sensitivity or emotional awareness of the impact his surprise announcement had on the team? A better understanding of the implications and impact of EI begins with a better understanding of the range of emotions that are present within us all. That brings us to the issue of how our emotions triggered in the first place.

In his book, *Emotional Intelligence 2.0*, Travis Bradberry starts with a look at the brain. In his view, before we can apply rational thought to a situation, that situation is first filtered through the emotional part of our brain. As a result, Bradberry says, our emotions influence everything we observe, say or do, and must be factored into the way we respond to any situation. In his book, the author explains how EI is the mediating force, or the filtering agent between the rational and emotional elements of our brain, referred to as the *limbic system*. "Emotional intelligence", the author states, "is the force that blends our emotional and rational thoughts into the way we respond and act towards others."

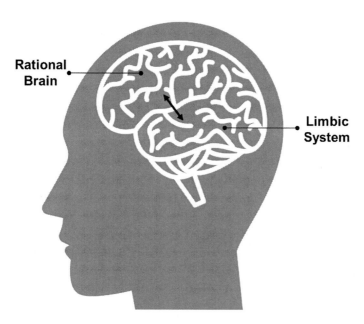

Rational Brain

Limbic System

Emotional intelligence is a balance between the rational and emotional brain

EI is what guides our responses when we have to balance the thoughts in our brain versus the feelings we may have about a particular issue. Emotional intelligence, a business professor once told his class, is not a matter of the heart governing the head. It is a matter of integrating rational thought (the head) with an understanding of what's going on with the other person (the heart).

So, how do we apply that head/heart process in our work setting, then at home or in other settings where a very different response may be required? Dorothy Rodwell, a mental health professional based in Fort Myers, Florida, recommends we use the concept referred to as "compartmentalization". She says that keeping your personal situation separate from your role as a leader and maintaining those firewalls can preserve your professionalism, and hence your leadership skill.

"The car broke down, the cat died, my son got in trouble at school, my boss is looking over my shoulder all the time, I can't pay my bills, and an important deadline is tomorrow." Whatever the situation at home, and there are many that confront us, the author says, compartmentalizing is a coping strategy that allows our minds to deal with conflicting internal emotions while simultaneously being able to lead."

The techniques for maintaining the emotional balance between our personal lives and our leadership responsibilities can vary widely... from compartmentalizing and completely separating the two, or to the other extreme of being fully disclosing about your personal matters to your team members. Whatever technique works best for you, it is important to not allow your personal life, be it your finances, the spouse, the kids or other aspects of your life, to interfere with your leadership.

Step 2—"Sense" Emotions

As leaders, our employees very seldom express their emotions directly. In more cases than not, that burden is ours. That is where the art of "sensing" comes into play. Our emotional intelligence doesn't tell us *what* to do; but it does provide guidance as to *how* to go about it.

For every action, every directive, every order, every command, every position we take as leaders, another human being is on the receiving end of that action. That human being is guided not by blind obedience because you're the boss, but by his or her emotions. Do I like my boss? Do I respect my boss? Do I trust my boss? What are my feelings about the situation? Are my feelings even considered? Does my opinion even matter?

All of those opinions and emotions impact productivity. Some of them are expressed verbally, but many times nonverbally. Through body language, eye contact or other means, we communicate how we are feeling.

Further, what is expressed is many times expressed, not to the leader, but to other team members. Leaders very seldom get their information about how their team is feeling verbally or directly. It is received via their personal antennae. We all have one. But leaders who have highly developed EI skills have cultivated theirs to a higher level. They are constantly in "sensing" mode. Both in one-on-one and group discussions, they hear what is being said and how it is being said. More importantly, they hear what is not being said. "A lack of enthusiasm", a leader once said, "is not stated verbally, but it is communicated, nonetheless!"

Leaders with high levels of EI can not only hear what is being said; they can hear what is *not* being said.

Your sensing skills, like all other aspects of EI, can be developed. The next time you are communicating with an individual or a group of individuals, in a business or a social setting, listen to what is not being said.

Whether collecting input, formulating strategy, giving directions, or just having a casual conversation with a colleague, boss or subordinate, your sensing skills will dictate the types of questions you will ask, influence what actions we take or don't take, and how vigorously we take them.

Bob Burke led a consulting group in a large firm and was considered an ideal employee and leader. His eleven-member team consistently rated him a "Five" on the company's semi-annual 5-Point Leadership scale. They frequently commented on his "personal interest in his employees" as well as his exceptional leadership skills. Bob was known for being actively engaged in the well-being of his employees and their families. From an EI perspective, Bob was off the charts.

One Monday morning, as the team gathered for their weekly staff meeting, Bob seemed distracted, irritable, and clearly not his usual engaging self. During the meeting, as other members of the team were enjoying their usual banter, Bob abruptly said, "Can we dispense with all the nonsense, and focus on business?" The room suddenly went silent. On any other occasion, Bob would have been the instigator of the personal banter during their meetings, so his somewhat gruff demeanor was clearly out of character. Something was amiss.

At the end of the meeting, Eric, one of Bob's senior team members who knew his boss both socially and professionally, stayed behind in the conference room with Bob.

"What's going on, boss? You seem a little out of sorts this morning," he said to his friend and boss.

"Eric," Bob reluctantly replied, "Deborah and I are getting a divorce.

We knew it was coming, but it all came to a head over the weekend, and I guess I brought it to work with me this morning. I didn't want to announce it in the meeting, but I will explain to the other team members at the appropriate time."

Eric displayed and acted on his sensing skills with his boss. He "heard" something unusual in Bob's behavior and had the courage to confront the situation.

Step 3—"Seek" Others' Emotions

Beyond the art of reading emotions nonverbally, or "sensing", direct questioning is an equally critical skill in EI. Morten needed to know how his team was feeling following his boss' surprise announcement. He was anxious to engage them directly, but this would require the right setting, being open to input from others, and very attentive listening . . . listening and observing. Morten knew that emotions are expressed both verbally and non-verbally, and reading both sets of cues would be essential? And, despite the potentially exciting news, not everyone would have the same feelings about the situation.

Morten's questioning skills and situational awareness would be tested. He remembered a class he once took on questioning techniques, and a tip his instructor gave him. "When the situation is emotionally charged," the instructor said, "you only need to ask one question . . . 'How are you feeling?' The respondent will take it from there.' Effective questioning is a vital EI skill.

Step 4—Know Your Setting and Your Audience

The situations listed in the chart below, 1x1, group setting or social setting, may serve as the foundation for how to apply your emotional intelligence; however, our business environment has become more complex. Age, culture and work settings are just a few of the different situations in which we find ourselves. Morten's boss is younger than he is. Does that make a difference in how he responds? His team members are of different cultures. Does that make a difference?

The more complex our business environments become, the more

situations we encounter, thus requiring more sophisticated approaches to EI. Different cultures, different generations, different settings all require a more nuanced approach. While the fundamental skills of EI remain largely the same, the variety of circumstances in which leaders find themselves, can call for a very different application of those skills.

As the chart below illustrates, there are multiple dimensions to consider. The setting, inside the workplace or outside should be considered. The age, race and culture of our audience should be considered. Even the issue of a face-to-face discussion versus one taking place over the phone is a factor.

Our work environment has become much more global and diverse, and the art and skill of EI has become more varied and multi-dimensional as a result.

Step 5—Know Your Environment

An extension of knowing your audience, is being aware of your circumstance or environment. Specifically, if you are dealing with someone one-on-one, you can engage more directly, more candidly, than in a group setting. The dynamics are different, and the emotions are more clear, as the chart below suggests.

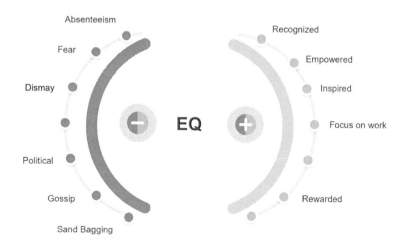

Potential Impact on Performance – 1 to 1

In contrast, a setting with multiple players, one-to-many, creates a dramatically different environment. People are generally less willing to reveal their emotions, whether verbally or nonverbally, and less inclined to engage in an emotional manner.

Your task in that situation is simply to be aware of the emotions of those around you. Whether they intend to or not, they will project some emotional affect. Their topic of conversation, alone, evokes some emotional clues. Your job is to sense them and engage accordingly.

What emotions, positive or negative, would the topics in the below graphic suggest? Developing your EI means learning to study and discern people's emotions.

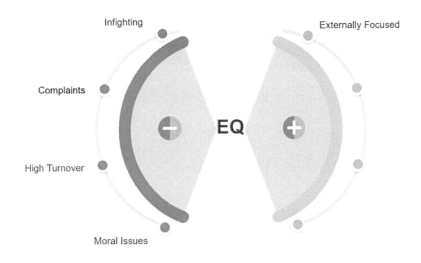

Infighting   Externally Focused

Complaints

EQ

High Turnover

Moral Issues

Potential Impact on Performance – 1 to Many

We know the audiences you engage on a day-to-day basis are typically varied, and in many cases, complex. Whether it is 1x1, 1xmany, your boss, your colleagues, older, younger, the same or a different culture, your EI is about sensing those emotions, being sensitive to them, and managing your communications accordingly.

The following chart illustrates just how varied and complex those circumstances can be.

	Age race culture Upward vs. Downward Internal vs. External		
	1 & 1	**1 & Many**	**1 & Social**
	Self Aware	Self Aware	Self Aware
What I see	xx	xx	xx
	xx	xx	xx
	xx	xx	xx
	xx	xx	xx
What I do	xx	xx	xx
	xx	xx	xx
	xx	xx	xx
	xx	xx	xx
	xx	xx	xx
What I need to do	xx	xx	xx
	xx	xx	xx
	xx	xx	xx
	xx	xx	xx
	xx	xx	xx

Workplace Dimensions

* * *

Morten also learned he would be asked to meet with the team leaders and their bosses from two outside groups that would now be potential partners for the upcoming presentation. He knew they may have the same apprehension and concerns that his own team had shared and would need to be sensitive to their concerns as well. But this would require a little more subtlety, depending on the person or persons with whom he would be interacting.

His empathy, listening skills and communication skills would all be tested. Whether they were his boss, a colleague or subordinate; and whether they were internal or external to his company, he had to be ready.

* * *

There are endless situations in our daily work lives that provoke emotions. Sometimes, they can be debilitating; sometimes they can be unpredictable; and sometimes invisible to the untrained eye. Further, they are not only provoked by major events such as the one Morten and his team encountered. From the daily stress that accompanies the work environment, to employee conflicts, to missed promotions, missed deadlines, or missed numbers, the daily encounters of the human experience, especially in the work setting, are challenges requiring emotional intelligence.

The concept of "management by walking around" was conceived as a direct response to the increased need for EI in the workplace. In addition to saying, "How's the project coming?" managers are now coached to add the question, "How are you doing?"

*   *   *

Step 6—Take Action

Having the sensitivity and emotional intelligence is necessary, but not sufficient, if you don't act on the situation; even if you're not in control of the situation. In some cases a leader has the power to resolve an issue. In other cases, the issue is beyond the control of both parties. In either circumstance, some form of action should always be taken to either bring the issue to a resolution, or simply demonstrate genuine sensitivity and caring for the situation.

As the following graphic illustrates, there are a variety of actions required to be "emotionally intelligent", all of which are essential in your ability to communicate, engage and lead others.

Seek Advice

Prepare

Understand Feelings
Your's & Others

Anticipate

Prepare Attendees

Manage Impulses

Energy Positive

Be Conscious of
Personal Brand

Acknowledge/Empathize

Control Negative
Thoughts

Calibrate

Practice, Practical,
Practice

Engagement framework for EQ – Mind Map

*   *   *

The following morning, Morten met with his team as planned and shared that "things were happening" that could be good for the team. Using the above chart, he recovered by creating a mind map of his actions and allowed the group members to vent during a Q&A discussion and stated he would like to meet with individuals separately, or in small groups to discuss the situation further. While working out schedules for the meetings, he learned that some of the team would be unavailable during the day and was asked if he would meet them after work instead. He agreed.

He wanted to provide the opportunity for everyone to get an update on the situation and at the same time, have the opportunity to express their feelings, but he knew different situations required different approaches.

*   *   *

Even when you're unable to fix the situation, simply being aware of another's situation and responding to their emotions, can be enough. Consider the case of Jim McNeil.

*   *   *

Jim McNeil was a project manager for a large multinational construction company. He was managing a large project in Taiwan with project team members from Australia, Japan, the Philippines, India, Taiwan and the U.S.

One morning while preparing his monthly report, Jim was approached by a member of his team from the Philippines who was visibly agitated. After Jim invited the team member into his office, the individual told him, "I was just informed that my visa has expired, and I would have to return to the Philippines to reapply for a new one." Knowing both the sensitivity and bureaucracy of international work visas, they both knew the situation could take months, virtually ending the employee's work on the project. Jim also knew this was above his paygrade, but felt he had to do something on his team member's behalf.

Jim immediately got on the phone. He made calls to his boss, the company's human resources director, his customer, and even the Taiwanese State Department. Eventually, it became apparent that the employee would indeed be required to return to his home country and reapply for his visa, thus putting his job in jeopardy. Jim was both frustrated and disappointed. His inability to resolve the situation would cause a disruption to his team's productivity and a have a severe impact on the employee's livelihood.

The employee sadly prepared for his departure back to his homeland. In an emotional exit questionnaire, the employee stated:

I am leaving my job not on my own accord and hope to return to complete my work with Jim McNeil and this project team. If I am unable to return, I can only hope to work for another supervisor who has the sensitivity and caring of Jim McNeil.

Neither Jim nor his supervisors were able to resolve this particular employee's situation. But the effort Jim put forth had an indelible impact on the employee. He demonstrated the sensitivity, urgency and emotional intelligence that would remain with his employee long after this project was completed.

Putting IQ and EQ Together

Each of the quotients we put forth in this book should not be viewed in isolation, but as an integrated system that collectively leads to lifetime employability.

They should be viewed in the same fashion of a baseball player collectively mastering the components of hitting, running, catching, and throwing. Though each component can be analyzed separately and can be trained separately it is when the baseball player takes the field that those components must work together as one integrated unit.

The same is true here, especially when you consider your IQ and EQ. We all know of individuals who are brilliant but without social skills; and we also know individuals who are just the opposite. As you saw in the previous segments, the absence of either can have an effect in terms of how we perform and how we are perceived.

The Impact of IQ and EQ on Your Performance

Those same domains serve as a basic benchmark of our ability to perform our jobs. Our work-related IQ, combined with our emotional intelligence join together, almost in binary terms, to project just how we will fare in the workplace. Consider the graphic below.

For example, someone with the golden characteristics of both a *high IQ and high EQ* is considered a rock star. They are individuals that demonstrate the abilities to lead and manage high-performance teams, and typically rise both within their own organization, and within their industry.

Those possessing a *high IQ, but low levels of emotional intelligence (EQ)*, however, typically possess a limiting ability to lead. Individuals with that combination of characteristics are typically better as individual contributors rather than leaders. If they do attain leadership positions, they typically stay there or revert back to becoming individual contributors.

In contrast, individuals possessing a *high EQ, but low IQ,* suggests something altogether different. It suggests they are surviving mostly on their charm, personality and engagement skills. With a limited range of intelligence, an individual could potentially maneuver his or her way through an organization up to a certain level, and then go into cruising mode. These are individuals that are characterized by the "Peter Principle".

Finally, as depicted in the lower, left quadrant, those who are *low both in IQ AND EQ* typically reside in the shadows of an organization. They are projected to be somewhat limited in their abilities to adequately perform their jobs, and in their abilities to engage effectively with others, hence the phrase, "Performance at Risk".

In which quadrant do you fit?

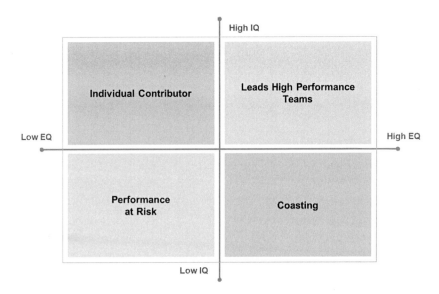

IQ Impact on Performance

The Impact of IQ and EQ on Your "Brand"

Our intelligence not only plays a major role in our leadership effectiveness and decision-making, it plays an equally critical role in how we are viewed by others. All of us possess a reputation in the workplace as it relates to our intelligence. All who have worked with us, our peers, our subordinates and our bosses, would have an opinion about us if pressed.

Again, in combination with our emotional intelligence, those opinions of our fellow workers serve as the formulation of our brand.

A high IQ combined with a high EQ again puts us in the rock star territory. Individuals possessing that rare combination are viewed as visionaries. They are capable of seeing things that do not yet exist and have the interpersonal attributes to enable others to see the same thing.

Those possessing a *high IQ, but low EQ* have many of the same visionary attributes minus the inter—or intra-personal capabilities to engage others. Theirs is a reputation or brand many describe as "eccentric".

Those on the *lower end of the IQ spectrum* are many times characterized as "low performers" or as simply a "nice people" depending on their levels of emotional intelligence.

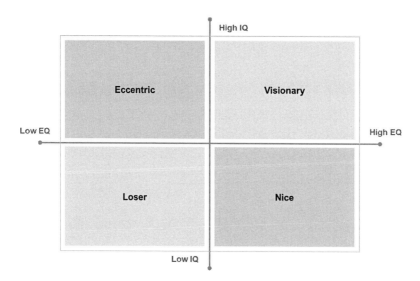

IQ Impact on Personal Brand

Conclusion

The significance of emotional intelligence as a leadership quality cannot be overstated, especially in the context of today's rollercoaster environment driven by globalization and digitization. Business leaders describe today's world of work in byzantine terms, such as schizophrenic and hyper-competitive both at the micro and macro levels, and far too obsessed with instant gratification.

The workplace is more virtual, transient and diverse than ever, requiring leaders and their employees to engage one another from a distance like never before, yet as if they are in the office next door. Additionally, social media further exacerbates the situation. Tools such as Facebook, Twitter and instant messaging give us the ability to connect, but not to engage.

Yet, in the midst of these impersonal headwinds, practitioners and behavioral scientists view EI as one of the top three qualities required of a leader; and many view it as the number one quality ranked even higher than intelligence, decisiveness or strategic thinking. EI requires a variety of skills and a constant sense of awareness, both qualities of which can be learned; but most of all, it requires a dedication to the wellbeing of your employees, both personally and professionally. That dedication must be reflected by practices and behaviors; and those behaviors are typically governed by guiding principles such as the following:

Guiding Principles

1. *Actively Engage*—Confront and embrace EI opportunities; do not shy away. This practice will internalize and you're your ability to address emotional or sensitive situations.

2. *Respond Immediately*—Emotions are now. Practice a sense of urgency, as opposed to waiting for a better time.

3. *Cultivate your network*—Prepare a nimble network of advisors you can call upon for different situations.

4. *Confirm the Facts*—Why? What? When? How? Know the cause and know the proposed resolution.

5. *Focus on the Goal*—Every situation has emotions, and every situation is tied to an intended objective. Respond to the emotions but focus on the goal.

6. *Move on*—Address the situation, then move on. Do not allow emotions to linger; do not gloat; do not sulk.

7. *Stay in the Present*—Yesterday's situation belongs to yesterday; not today.

8. *Master the Analytics*—Social media and other tools provide analytics to enhance EI. Learn them and use them.

9. *Shift the Balance*—Negative emotions are typically expressed more than positive ones. In those circumstances, shift the balance from the negative to the positive by accentuating successes.

10. *Invest, Learn and Practice*—Make EI an integral part of your interactions.

CHAPTER 3
LQ—Learning Quotient

Textbooks will become obsolete, replaced by Netflix-style education and a focus on 'how to learn' rather than 'what to learn'

—Manish Bahl

Introduction

To complete the foundational elements of your "house of lifetime employability" we pose the question, *how well are you able to learn, unlearn and relearn?* That, along with your IQ and EQ, collectively serve as your foundation, especially in this era of rapid change and disruption.

There was a time when jobs remained fairly constant. From auto mechanics to dental hygienists to IBM computer programmers, the process, the technology, and the word was generally the same at the end of their careers as it was in the beginning. Changes occurred slowly. New concepts or technologies were introduced gradually. Employees were given the benefit of the time and detailed instruction to absorb new practices.

That world is no longer. The pace of change mirrors the pace of innovations in technology. Those who complain or reminisce of how "things aren't like they used to be" are left in the same trash heap as rotary phones and fax machines. The ability to learn, unlearn and relearn new processes, new technologies, new practices, has become an essential element of lifetime employability. And for that reason, we view it as part of the foundation in our construct of the house of leadership.

At its forefront is technology. And as if we need any further evidence of how technology is changing every facet of our society, the very process of learning, of securing and maintaining an education serves as its own exhibit. The concepts of what we learn and how we learn are being transformed at lightning speed.

A little background . . .

Education, as we know it today, is rooted in the late 19th and early 20th centuries. The significance of that timing is that it was structured to support the Industrial Revolution. Now the world is global, multidisciplinary, massively networked, and hypercomplex. It was not too long ago, for instance, that the process of learning began with the basics of math, science, language and history. We then advanced to learning the subjects related to our vocations and careers. After that was completed, we went to work. Our "continuing education" consisted primarily of what was required to remain current in our chosen career field. And all that learning took place in a physical classroom, lecture hall, laboratory or auditorium.

Today, that learning process begins in the same fashion, but from there, both the content and the methods of learning are being re-engineered to reflect today's technology and work environment.

That classroom or lecture hall is now no further away than our fingertips, and available to us from the comfort of our living room or den. Our professor and classmates can be next door or on another continent. Online, or distance learning has advanced from being a novelty viewed as lesser quality or prestige to becoming the norm. The prestigious Harvard Medical School, for example, is now offering its postgraduate medical education for physicians, researchers, and other health care providers, online.

Its brochure states, "many of our programs leverage a blended learning approach, which combines live and web-based class sessions, interactive group assignments, and one-on-one access to Harvard Medical School faculty. The duration of programs varies from a few days to a two-year master's degree. This allows clinicians, clinical scientists, and clinical administrators to choose what meets their career needs and work schedule." Their programs do not consist of professors conducting "lectures" to impart knowledge, but a learning experience of "guided discovery." The professor's job is to guide and direct the learning experience, but the learning process itself, now belongs to the student. Additionally, that textbook which has traditionally contained the content for learning, has now been displaced by electronic archives.

Given the rapid and continuous changes in technology, and therefore in the marketplace and in our jobs, the learning process which was once viewed as a one-time preparatory event, is now a lifetime cyclical endeavor of learning, unlearning and relearning. With the information increasingly accessible electronically, combined with technologies such as artificial intelligence (AI), virtual reality (VR) and augmented reality (AR), lifelong, individualized learning is now the norm.

To support this growing phenomenon of lifelong learning, according to Manish Bahl, Vice President of the Center for the Future of Work, "companies must create a culture of learning so that individuals are self-motivated and curious to acquire new skills, while upgrading the existing ones."

Today's technologies are rendering business processes, and in some cases, jobs and businesses of yesterday, obsolete. Tomorrow's technologies will have the same impact on what we know today. Your learning quotient (LnQ), your ability to learn, unlearn and relearn new technologies, new concepts and new business practices, stands at the forefront of your lifetime employability.

LQ Defined

Your Learning Quotient, or LnQ, is defined as:

Your desire and ability to grow and adapt to new technologies, new concepts, new practices and new environments.

Developing your *LQ* is best encapsulated in the formula,

IT2—Invest in tomorrow's technologies.

Your LQ

Your LQ and your ability to increase your LQ, is contingent on seven elements:

1. *Your acceptance or beliefs about learning.* Your epistemological view that learning is the centerpiece of progress and advancement, is fundamental to your ability to learn and relearn.

2. *Your persistence* in seeking out new concepts, new ideas, or new technologies.

3. *Your ability to change* or unlearn.

4. *Your ability to self-teach*, or learn on your own.

5. *Your determination*, or intent to learn.

6. *Your ability to learn in groups*, from and with others.

7. *Your ability and willingness to employ various tools of learning*, such as audio or visual devices.

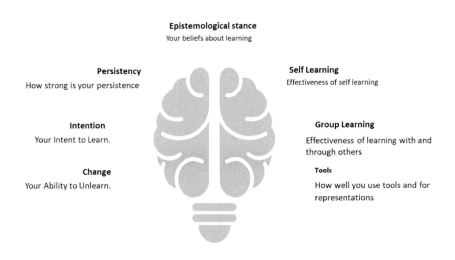

Epistemological stance
Your beliefs about learning

Persistency
How strong is your persistence

Self Learning
Effectiveness of self learning

Intention
Your Intent to Learn.

Group Learning
Effectiveness of learning with and through others

Change
Your Ability to Unlearn.

Tools
How well you use tools and for representations

The 7 Learning Elements across the Learning Environment

Methods of Lifelong Learning

As there are prerequisites to lifelong learning, there are also various methods one should be adept at to accommodate that learning.

Self-Learning, Unsupervised

As cited previously, much of today's learning will be self-learning, or unsupervised learning. In a growing number of instances, the burden to learn new processes or new technologies will be ours.

If the icemaker on my refrigerator is broken, and I wish to replace it without the expense of a plumber, fortunately, the burden is mine to learn how to do it. Fortunately, the step-by-step process of how to do it is at my fingertips through the magic of YouTube.

Similarly, in the workplace, if I want to learn how to calculate my business expenses more efficiently, the same technologies are available to me is at my fingertips.

Supervised Learning

In other instances, the burden of learning remains my own, but can be delivered with the help or supervision of another.

An example of this type of *supervised learning* is if your company is implementing a new application, such as an ERP system like Salesforce, however, classes will most likely be conducted under the supervision of a Salesforce or IT representative. That class can be conducted in an actual classroom or remotely in a virtual classroom.

Your guidance may be supervised, but the burden to focus and learn is your own.

Reinforced Learning

A third method of learning, be it supervised or unsupervised, can be *reinforced learning.* You may be pursuing a diploma or a certification, such as an MBA or a real estate license, or may be required to maintain a certification through continuing educations credits such as a medical professional or an IT professional, or an accountant.

This type of reinforced learning is typically applied when a certain set of standards are required to be met and maintained.

Using each of these methods, the burden of seeking the knowledge is shifting from the corporation to the individual. It is the lifelong learner who will comfortably prosper and learn in this new environment.

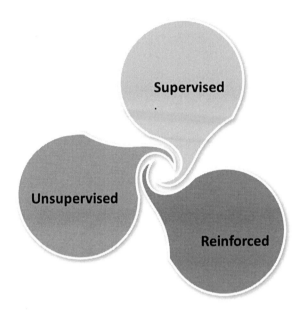

The Learning Methods

How Your LQ Impacts Your Performance

Your performance is incumbent upon being abreast of the latest trends, the latest practices and the latest technologies, all of which are subject to change from day to day. When you are operating on yesterday's news, you are relying on past performances . . . the way things used to be done as opposed to the way they are being done today, or will be done tomorrow

The pace of change is accelerating at an unprecedented rate as are the changes in practices to stay in sync with those changes. Annual updates have become quarterly. Updates to applications are occurring monthly if not more frequently. How frequently do you get updates for your iPhone or iPad, or other technologies? The changes that used to occur every six or twelve months, are now happening monthly.

Top performers are lifelong learners . . . continually curious and continually looking forward. They are less interested in the way things used to be done, and more interested in how they will be done.

How Your LQ Impacts Your Brand

You know the people who are up-to-date on the latest business practices. You know the ones who are tech savvy and can guide you. You know the individuals who are in sync with industry or competitive trends

Those are the ones whose personal brand includes being "in the know".

Conversely, you know the ones who don't have a clue. You know the ones who are still asking their secretary to help them fill out an expense report or a sales report. You know the ones who are still using flip phones because they are "simpler to operate". You know the ones who freak out when the boss asks them to provide a competitive update. Those are the ones whose brand reflects *not* being "in the know".

Chances are you reside somewhere in between that spectrum. And know that you are perceived to be somewhere in that spectrum. Wherever that is, that's your brand. Your colleagues know it and your boss knows it.

And your assignments, your promotions, and your sustained employment hangs in the balance. What's your LQ Brand?

Developing Your LQ

Developing your LQ comes down to two basic questions:

1. *What do I need to know?*

2. *How do I obtain it?*

Let's take each of those one at a time.

What I need to know?

This question can be broken down into three parts:

- *What do I need to know to perform now?*

  This question is akin to basketball player simply trying to make the team. You may be on the team, but you are not assured of being in the starting line-up, and certainly with no assurances of becoming a superstar. Marshall Goldsmith, a well renowned coach in business consultant, wrote a book entitled, *What Got You Here Will Not Get You There.* In it, he chronicles several "C" Level individuals whose careers stalled when they relied on past practices as their guide going forward.

  Whatever skills, attributes and knowledge you need to perform adequately in your current job, there are no assurances that those same skills and knowledge will take you further.

- *What do I need to know to advance further and be promoted?*

  This is a more ambitious question and will take you further into the realm of continuous learning, both in terms of content and process. This will require you to look beyond your current job to anticipate what your future job will require of you. It essentially puts you in the position of operating on two parallel tracks: learning what is required of you in your current job, while concurrently learning about your next job.

  It is from this vantage point that you begin to understand those who spend inordinate time with their boss. They may not be suck-up's as you may have suspected. They may merely be trying to develop a better understanding of the nuances at the next level.

- *What do I need to know to assure myself of lifetime employability?*

Now you are in the realm of the superstar. That individual is studying business trends, new technologies, the factors that are driving the company's stock price, the critical drivers of revenue and profitability, and more. That individual is clicking on all the Q's and continuously learning what is happening today, tomorrow, and two years down the road.

What is your response when you ask the question, "what do I need to know?"

How do I obtain that information?

Once you answer the first question, your next question is the *how*!

As we discussed previously, the learning forum was at one point a classroom. Today, that classroom is a virtual classroom. It is your own personal *learning hub*, which is a rich career repository of curricula and resources, ranging from Googled information, TED talks, YouTube video presentations, tools and job aides; complimented by your own private network of coaches, mentors and social media connections.

Your mentors and coaches are there to guide you in shaping your curriculum, in other words, your pathways to your learning repository. Your tools, presentations and repositories are your sources; and, your social network is there to help you expand and enrich those sources.

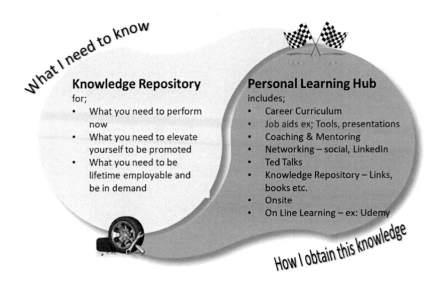

What I need to know

Knowledge Repository
for;
- What you need to perform now
- What you need to elevate yourself to be promoted
- What you need to be lifetime employable and be in demand

Personal Learning Hub
includes;
- Career Curriculum
- Job aids ex; Tools, presentations
- Coaching & Mentoring
- Networking – social, LinkedIn
- Ted Talks
- Knowledge Repository – Links, books etc.
- Onsite
- On Line Learning – ex: Udemy

How I obtain this knowledge

Develop Learning Quotient

Summary

As evidenced in virtually every aspect of what we do and how we do it, combined with the mind-bending innovations in technology, the need for continuous, lifelong learning is more essential than ever. Fortunately, the tools and resources necessary to support that learning are more prevalent than ever.

Architecture is no longer just about designing buildings. It is about designing buildings factoring in the ecological, environmental, and sustainability conditions that must accompany that design. Medicine is no longer just about anatomy. It is about the microorganisms and their pharmacological implications, stem cells, and non-invasive, robotic surgical techniques.

As technology drives the growing complexities of the workplace, so grow the demands of learning at the same pace. Fortunately, the methods and technologies of the learning process are keeping pace. Now, it is our jobs to do the same.

Knowing the right skills and attributes, for today and tomorrow, and how to develop them is one part of that job. Having the attitude and commitment to lifelong learning is the other. Lifelong learning requires a collection of skills, attitudes, attributes and behaviors to drive its thirst and its objectives.

Having to learn the latest version of your accounting software is the equivalent of having to retake calculus for the second and third time. Doing that repeatedly can be tedious and deflating without the right attitude.

To the individual that is only concerned with staying current with their present job, the process is wearing. To the individual concerned about lifetime employability, the process is welcoming.

What once was an occasional perusal on the web or a seminar at a conference, is now a steady diet of learning, unlearning and relearning as technology continues to drive new innovations, new practices and new markets.

That process encompasses a variety of disciplines, as the below graphic suggests. Our new environment of continuous learning requires them all.

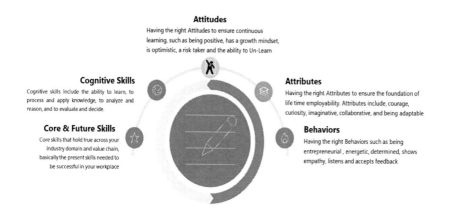

Attitudes
Having the right Attitudes to ensure continuous learning, such as being positive, has a growth mindset, is optimistic, a risk taker and the ability to Un-Learn

Cognitive Skills
Cognitive skills include the ability to learn, to process and apply knowledge, to analyze and reason, and to evaluate and decide.

Attributes
Having the right Attributes to ensure the foundation of life time employability. Attributes include, courage, curiosity, imaginative, collaborative, and being adaptable

Core & Future Skills
Core skills that hold true across your industry domain and value chain, basically the present skills needed to be successful in your workplace

Behaviors
Having the right Behaviors such as being entrepreneurial, energetic, determined, shows empathy, listens and accepts feedback

Having the right mindset for learning

Guiding Principles

1. Establish your personal Learning Hub
2. Be hungry to learn.
3. Attend seminars, TED talks, etc.
4. Take a lead from your Leaders' learning efforts.
5. Learn to unlearn.
6. Develop your cognitive skills.
7. Seek opportunities to invest in learning
8. Devote 2% + in annual salary in your learning hub.
9. To learn more effectively . . . teach others!
10. Learn from Your Customer

PART II

The Pillars

A foundation is just that . . . a base from which to build the pillars of success. The second "P" is performance, the attributes necessary to consistently perform at a high level.

CHAPTER 4
XQ—Execution Quotient

A S WE MOVE beyond the foundation of your House of Lifetime Employability, we examine its pillars which further sustain your viability in the workplace, how you are valued, and your ability to sustain your career. That begins with your ability to do what you say you'll do . . . your ability to execute!

In our previous book, the *'Me' Enterprise*, we describe four elements of leadership responsibilities as:

1. *Strategy*—The ability to formulate a winning strategy or game plan

2. *Execution*—The ability to execute that game plan

3. *Technology*—The ability to leverage technology as a differentiator, and,

4. *Governance*—The ability to ensure proper governance and oversight of the planning and execution of the business.

This chapter is about the second of those four elements—execution.

Execution Quotient (XQ)—Your Execution Quotient (XQ), simply put, is your ability to consistently deliver or exceed expectations as it relates to your performance.

Your Execution Quotient (*XQ*) is exactly what the title suggests . . . your ability to deliver results! Whether you are a sales executive with a revenue quota, a project manager measured on delivering on time, on budget, and to specification or a finance analyst responsible for compiling the financial results at quarter's end; if you are unable to deliver the results, the other quotients will not matter.

There is an expression in sales that says, "if you have the numbers, you don't need to talk much." The simple translation: if you deliver the results, the numbers speak for themselves. The inverse of that expression is that sales executives who *don't* meet their quota, wind up doing a lot of explaining, justifying, and tap dancing. Tap dancers don't last very long in the business world.

In our previous book, we defined your ability to execute in accordance to your metrics as one of the major components for surviving in the business world. We wrote:

> *"Every leader is ultimately judged on accomplishments. When a prospective employer looks at your resume, or interviews you for a prospective opportunity, the vetting process begins there in order to assess your effectiveness . . . What have you accomplished?"*

Execution and your execution quotient (*XQ*) are all about performance.

With the combination of technology and improved analytics, even the softest of performance expectations are now quantifiable. Sales professionals live and die by their numbers. They know how many sales calls they are expected to make each quarter; they know how many of those calls they are expected to close and they know what their personal sales commissions will be when they close the deal.

For those who work in other areas such as manufacturing, operations or human resources, their measure of success was in many cases, subjective. How do you measure issues such as customer satisfaction or employee engagement? Those activities within an organization that were once considered soft or unmeasurable can now be quantified and converted to numbers. Those employees may not know their numbers, but they exist nonetheless, and those individuals are being judged accordingly.

A manufacturing employee's number may be the number of units produced, or the number of factory rejects that are received. A human resources employee may be judged on number of employee interviews or hires, or number of performance appraisal interviews conducted. And the employee in accounting may be measured on the number of reports produced, or the number of errors that are found in those reports.

Whatever job you have in your company, you can be assured you have a number. Your ability to execute begins with knowing that number(s), embracing it. That is your measure of execution. Whatever your job and however you are measured, expect your boss to preach three things:

1. Numbers

2. NUMBERS

3. **NUMBERS!**

Somebody's Watching You!

Whatever your number and wherever you work, you can safely assume that someone is keeping track of your numbers. If you're not aware of your number, you can be assured someone in your organization is. Whether it be through a sophisticated ERP program displaying an employee dashboard, such as below, or on the back of a napkin, your performance is being monitored.

If your company does employ an ERP system, such as Salesforce, SAP or Oracle, that typically means that you have visibility to the same dashboard your boss is monitoring. You should be monitoring it, also. First, you want to ensure it is accurate and up to date. Secondly, you want to be prepared to discuss any aspect of your dashboard when asked.

Golden Rule: Assume your boss knows your number and your current performance against that number as well as you do.

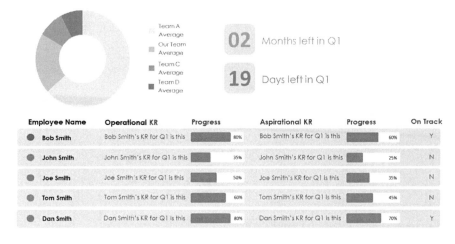

Performance Dashboard

Managing Your Number

So, how do you manage your number? Even if you are not measured strictly by numbers, you should create your own numerical metric. With that, what is the best way to actually achieve your number, both for yourself and your team? That process is typically a collection of four activities:

- *Negotiating and Collaborating Goals*
- *Inspiring and Encouraging Performance*
- *Managing Performance, and*
- *Compensating*

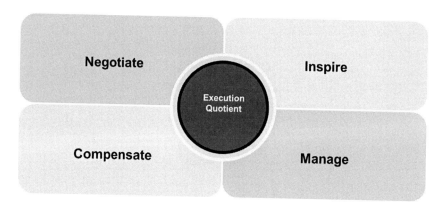

Execution Quotient

Let's examine each of the four major elements of effective execution, beginning with the first question . . . *How is your number established?*

Negotiate—The Politics of Metrics

If you have been the subject of a performance appraisal review, then you have most likely experienced the politics of goalsetting.

Goalsetting is a process that begins at the top and cascades downward throughout the organization. The process may have begun in the boardroom between shareholders and the CEO. It may have begun with the CEO acting arbitrarily. However, those expectations were conceived, that process begins at the top and cascades down to everyone in the organization. And somewhere in each of those expectations, your number(s) emerge.

If you are in sales, for example, and your sales manager is given a target of fifty sales for the quarter, and he has a team of five sales professionals, it is reasonable to expect that each of those salespersons will be given a number of ten sales each.

Knowing that some sales representatives may not be able to achieve their target of ten, it is also reasonable to expect the sales manager to build in an insurance policy by padding those numbers. He or she might give each salesperson an additional, stretch target to accommodate the potential shortfall and still achieve the group number.

Goalsetting is ultimately an exercise in numbers. It is also an exercise in negotiations.

Your boss wants you to deliver ten sales this quarter. However, you're in a tough market and believe you can only deliver six. The back and forth exercise results, let's say, in you getting a reduced sales target for the quarter of eight.

Now, the boss has accepted a target of fifty sales with his boss and assumed those fifty sales would be distributed down to each of his sales representatives. If you can only deliver eight and not ten, the boss has to find out where those other two sales can be made up. The negotiations continue . . .

Whether you are in sales, manufacturing, accounting, or human resources, the process is the same, and can be translated to numbers.

The exercise to establish your number is usually one of negotiations. Executing that number, however, is not. Whatever target you signed up for is what you will be measured against and judged as to your ability to execute.

Getting the 'Right' Numbers

Negotiating the right number for the upcoming month, quarter or year is always an interesting exercise. Sometimes the process is highly subjective, and sometimes it is arbitrary. Getting to the right number is invariably a process of give and take. But in getting there, look out for two dynamics . . . *Sandbagging* and *Watermelon metrics.*

If you lobby that your number should be 10%, but the market is growing at a rate of 25%, you are sandbagging. Your number should stretch your performance, be achievable, and be consistent with market expectations. If you lobby for a low number when the market is growing at a much higher level, it suggests to your boss that you are trying to coast and simply take advantage of market conditions.

That is never good.

On the other extreme if your boss is pushing a higher number in a slow growing or declining market, that can be what is referred to as Watermelon Metrics, which are those that look nice and green and impressive on the outside. But they are red and potentially dangerous on the inside.

If we set a goal of 10% growth for this quarter, but the market is growing at a rate of only 2%, we have created the perfect formula for failure.

Though a 10% growth metric looks appealing on paper, both to customers and shareholders, we and our employees are setting ourselves up to fail. When we fail to execute that number, we look bad and our employees become disillusioned, disgruntled, and are soon in the market for a new job.

While it is always good to stretch yourself and your employees to achieve results that exceed expectations, first and foremost, the results we pursue should be attainable.

Typically, the goalsetting process is governed by three questions:

1. *What is realistically achievable?*

2. *What will stretch the employee's performance?*

3. *What is going on in the marketplace?*

Many companies employ the practice of establishing two sets of metrics, one that is reasonable to expect (*the right number*); and a second that could be achieved assuming an ideal set of circumstances (*the best number*). Those are generally referred to as "stretch" or "aspire" goals.

When negotiating your deliverables or numbers for the quarter or year, think in terms of those two numbers: (1) your target, which with hard work, could reasonably be achieved; and (2) your "aspire" or "stretch" target, that which could be achieved if everything fell perfectly into place.

Executing against your metrics is reasonable and to be expected. Executing to your aspire target would be outstanding!

Executing, above all, begins with knowing and embracing your number.

Inspire

Whether giving or receiving an assigned number, the higher the likelihood of you executing against that number is dependent upon whether the process was collaborative or arbitrary.

As a boss, the process of assigning a number to an employee is easy; the process of getting the employee to embrace that number as his or her own, is a little more involved. As an employee, you want to have some say in the number you accept.

Therefore, the next rule serves as a principle between employer and employee.

> *Golden Rule: The more an employee is involved in determining their number (or metric), the greater the likelihood that employee will own that number, embrace it as their own, and execute.*

As the boss, you can never be certain an employee is going to make his or her number. But you can be certain that if an employee is given their number in an arbitrary fashion, the likelihood of making that number goes down significantly. As the employee on the receiving end of a number, if you do not truly embrace your number, it's only natural that you are less inclined to achieve it.

Goalsetting should be a collaborative process. The more you as an employee are involved in setting your goals, the more you will treat that goal as your own, and the likelihood of success increases. That same principle is true throughout the execution process.

"Coaching Up"

As an employer or boss, you will continually face challenges in getting your employees to consistently meet their assigned targets. As an employee, you will at times struggle to meet your targets. How you respond or how your boss responds to those situations is critical.

Clint Anderson was the Regional Sales Manager with a team of seventeen Account Managers. Clint had negotiated his quarterly Regional sales target with his boss that included a major win he was expecting from one of his Account Managers. Clint and his Account Manager had already agreed that the likelihood of winning this deal was high, and both had agreed to include the opportunity as part of their number.

As the quarter progressed, it became apparent that the opportunity both were counting on would not happen. Both Clint and his Account Manager were at risk of missing their quarterly forecasts. The Account Manager was devastated, and Clint was bitterly disappointed. This was not the first miss for this Account Manager and Clint was considering some form of corrective action for the Account Manager.

Yet, the Account Manager, Clint believed, was a good one. He had a good relationship with his customers and was competing in a very difficult market. Clint knew he had to stand behind his people, including this Account Manager, despite the disappointing loss.

At the next weekly sales meeting, Clint announced the loss of the opportunity, and said to the rest of the team:

This past week, we learned that the big opportunity David (the Account Manager) and the rest of us were counting on for this quarter, is not going to happen. There were circumstances beyond our control that caused us to lose this opportunity.

Every one of you, at one time or another, have been in the position that David is in now. And he did his part to help bail us out. It is our turn now to bail David out.

While we are working on a recovery plan, please let me know any additional opportunities that you have in your pipeline that may help compensate for this loss.

Thanks guys. We need your help.

As disappointed as Clint was, he was determined to stand by his Account Manager and his team. Though David may have fallen short this time, Clint knew there had been times in the past and there would be times in the future when he would need David to help bail out one of his teammates.

He remembered the expression his sales manager used to tell him,

Don't fire them. Fire them up!

Compensate

Contrary to conventional wisdom, our paycheck is not the sole, or even primary factor, that causes us to stay in our current position or leave to seek greener pastures.

If we feel we are being compensated fairly (in terms of the marketplace or others doing similar work), issues such as doing interesting work, being challenged, learning new things, etc., are far more determining factors, studies show.

So, in line with the below golden rule, the employee who is satisfied with their working conditions, including compensation, is the employee who is most likely to execute. See if this applies to you:

> *Golden Rule: Compensation alone does not cause an employee to leave their company. Being unfairly compensated with unreasonable expectations will.*

The corollary to that golden rule is, the more you are able to execute to or go beyond your targets, the more valuable you are to the company and the more leverage you have regarding your personal compensation.

Compensation, like lifetime employability, is a function of value, and is governed ultimately by your ability to execute.

In the increasingly competitive and challenging business environment, managers cannot afford to carry the employee who is unable to execute. Their loyalty is to talent and ability to execute, not people!

Manage: Getting the Desired Results

Once your number(s) is established, and you embrace it as your own, that number should become yours and your boss' singular focus. Sales professionals live and die with their numbers. They can tell you if they are below target, on target, or ahead of target. They can tell you their objectives for the day at breakfast time and tell you if they achieved those objectives at dinner that night.

Effective managers behave the same way, whether they have five employees or fifty employees. The good ones know each and every one of their employees' number; how they are performing against those numbers; and, what they have to do by the end of the months/quarters/years to meet their targets.

In every conversation you have with your boss, be it formal or informal, over dinner that night, or at a party, be expected to discuss your numbers ... your current status with your numbers, and the prospects of achieving them.

Establish a Pattern

The underlying theme of this book is how things are changing at an increasing rate of speed. Organizations change. Mergers and acquisitions are increasing. Bosses come and go. People get transferred. Markets ebb and flow.

Organizations are a flurry of constantly shifting tides.

That can mean the number you negotiated with your previous boss has to be renegotiated with your new boss. It could mean your new boss knows nothing about your history other than today. You could be a consistently excellent performer and hitting a rough patch in the market at the same time you have a new boss.

Successful execution is not a one-time event. Successful execution is a consistent pattern of success, from year-to-year, quarter-to-quarter.

In those discussions about your execution with a new boss, or a new division, or a new company, be prepared to discuss not just what you done in the last month or quarter, but consistently over a period of quarters or years.

And if you experienced a blip in your performance (which we always do), be equally prepared to discuss market conditions or other extenuating circumstances if they existed.

Hiring managers are not necessarily impressed by your performance over one quarter for one year. They are impressed by a consistent pattern of successful execution.

Know Your Boss' Numbers

There is an additional element to knowing and executing your own numbers and that is knowing your boss' numbers. Successful employees not only know and embrace their own number; they do the same with their boss' numbers.

The more you embrace your numbers and performance against those numbers, the greater the likelihood of you meeting or exceeding those numbers. The more you know and help your boss execute their numbers, the more you are valued and assured of having a place in the organization.

Whether in sales, manufacturing human resources, or accounting, you should adopt the same mantra as your boss . . . *numbers, numbers, numbers!*

If You're Going to Miss . . .

The *second worst* thing you can do in any organization, as it relates to execution, is not make your number. The *worst* thing you can do is to know you are not going to make your number and fail to let your manager know before it is too late to do anything about it.

To miss your objective on a rare occasion is understandable. We have all been there, we have all done it.

If and when you discover that a sale is not going to happen, or a report is not going to get in on time, or if there is a breakdown in the supply chain which is going to result in you or someone missing their number, there is a rule for how to handle that situation:

Golden Rule: *If you or someone in your group is going to miss completing an objective, notify your boss immediately.*

The only thing your boss hates more than missing his or her number, is being surprised about someone missing their number. Being notified early (1) gives your boss and opportunity to try to make up the miss with someone else and (2) gives him or her ample opportunity to alert *their* boss of a potential miss. The only cardinal sin worse than missing your number is surprising your boss with that news before they've had a chance to adjust.

Internal Abyss

Before we discuss those four critical elements, we are compelled to reiterate something else we spoke at length about in the *'Me' Enterprise*. It is something which can derail the most determined employee.

In our previous publication, we cited one of the biggest deterrents to execution as being what we called the "Internal Abyss". The internal, or administrative abyss, as described below, is a paradoxical phenomenon in which the more successful you become, or the higher you go into in organization, the more administrative work you assume. That typically translates into more reports, more presentations, and more time and energy spent reporting on and explaining your successful performance, or lack of. You can get caught in the trap of talking about your last success more than you do executing your next success.

If you are a successful performer, it can become an inevitable phenomenon, especially as you move up in the organization. So, a critical component of execution is to avoid or keep to an absolute minimum, these internal, noncustomer focused activities.

If you're an up-and-comer, you want to brag on your success. If you're a marginal performer, your bosses want to know what you're doing to improve. Either end of that reporting and presentation spectrum can lead to the Internal Abyss. Avoid at all costs.

Administrative (or Internal) Abyss (n)—A phenomenon, typically found in corporations, in which leaders whose primary expertise and value to their company is their customer-based activities, are gradually lulled into taking on more administrative responsibilities, at the expense of their customer—focused responsibilities, thus diminishing their individual competitive edge, and their value to their company.

Summary

Execution is perhaps the simplest and most straightforward of all the quotients necessary to sustain lifetime employability . . . it is about achieving or exceeding expectations.

Knowing your number, knowing your boss' number, meeting your expectations, helping others meet their expectations, and providing an early warning if you or anyone is at risk of achieving those expectations. Those are the key ingredients of being able to execute.

They are also the keys to delivering value and assuring your lifetime employability.

Guiding principles:

1. *Think . . . perform or perish!*

2. *Loyalty is assigned to talent, not people.*

3. *Get results ethically!*

4. *Digitize your execution (ERP systems; smart contacts, etc.)*

5. *Maintain your external focus.*

6. *Create new knowledge—Drive towards IP or new knowledge.*

7. *Work to help your boss make his/her numbers.*

8. *Beware of watermelon metrics.*

9. *Seek autonomy with accountability.*

10. *Numbers-Numbers-Numbers!*

CHAPTER 5
NQ—Networking Quotient

Being successful in this world is part what you know, and part who you know. You need both.

THE SECOND OF the Pillars has less to do with your ability to execute, but your ability to engage others and the ability to forge strong networks.

In this technology driven climate, when we think "networks" we tend to think of the software that links one computer to another, or your iPhone connection to your provider and other phones. In this case, however, we are referring to networks of *people*, not technical networks.

This chapter is about the network of relationships you create and maintain in your business and personal life that are critical to your sustained success. Your core skills, your domain expertise and your technical prowess is about *what* you know . . . networking is about *who* you know.

If we were to chart the factors that represent the collection of ingredients essential to lifetime employability, and rank their criticality, it would track something like this . . .

- *What you know*—(Your knowledge)   *25%*
- *Interpersonal skills* (How you engage others)   *25%*
- *The Strength of your Relationships*   *50%*

This, in no way is to suggest the first two categories are not critical in terms of you maintaining your competitiveness in today's marketplace. It is, however, to suggest that in that marketplace where a career spans twenty, thirty, or even forty years or more, you will engage an array of different companies and yet to be discovered business opportunities. And, assuming the other two categories, it is your network that will sustain you through that maze.

In *The Emergence of the 'Me' Enterprise*, we wrote about the marketplace of the 1960's and 70's where many employees spent their entire careers with a single company. That is not, nor is it likely to be, the marketplace of the 21ˢᵗ Century. The average length of time with a single company was once fifteen to thirty years, today is less than three.

As technology and competition are fueling new business opportunities and new companies at an unprecedented rate, they are also rendering other companies and industries obsolete at the same rate. To stay abreast of those changes and opportunities, whether within or outside your current company, maintaining a network of peers, colleagues, mentors and former bosses is more critical than ever.

As the chart below would suggest, we have long analyzed and tracked the significance, the scope and the process of developing and maintaining a strong personal, professional and social network. Our relationships are the lifeblood of our families, our friendships, and our success in business.

From our bosses and co-workers to our neighbors, and sometimes from the least likely sources, our careers and opportunities are influenced not just by what we know, but also who we know. Developing, nurturing and maintaining that network is an essential ingredient to lifetime employability.

Circle of influence

If you are like most, you have a wide circle of friends, co-workers, and acquaintances. And knowing that career advancement can come from virtually any of those sources, it would be easy to consider all of them your network. Our goal, however, is to become a little more discriminating when we consider who is or is not a part of our network.

When you consider the network of individuals that support you can add value to your career, think in terms of all those relationships, and then begin to narrow them down to a more select few. Somewhere amongst all of them is an inner circle of individuals that can truly be of value, and truly be regarded as your network.

Think of your network in these terms:

Networking Quotient (NQ): Your ability to cultivate and maintain a collection of friends, colleagues and leaders who are influential in guiding and coaching you throughout your career.

The Networking Value Chain

From a macro view, the art of professional networking has its own value chain. There are different types of networks that take different forms. There is the process of creating, nurturing, and maintaining networks. Then, there are the various tools by which to do so. Networking is an ecosystem in and of itself, within the galaxy of ecosystems that collectively result in lifetime employability.

The individual who has mastered this crucial art flows through its entities and components the way a concert pianist flows through a masterful composition.

From the types of networks you create to the tools you employ to engage them, the value chain below represents a comprehensive view of the various elements in creating and maintaining your network.

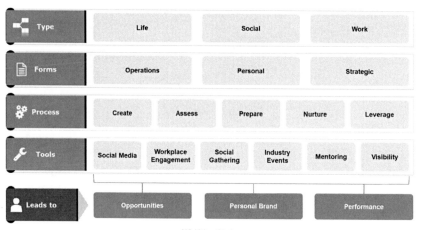

NQ Value Chain

As in virtually every facet of our experiences and our learnings, we tend to analyze it and break it down into an illustration of some sort. Networking is no different. In accordance with the following illustration, who amongst your friends and colleagues fit within the inner circle? They are your Power Base.

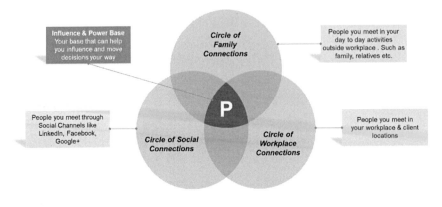

PowerBase Circles

Your Network

Or, to look at it another way, consider this . . . within that inner circle, think for a moment about the people you know that are, or could be, influential in your career. Now, think about the individuals that you have not yet engaged that *could* be very helpful and influential in your career. Now, how would you plot those individuals on the following graph? Are they influential? Are they potentially willing to help advance your career? Or, are they not in a position to help advance your career? Are they unwilling or uninterested? Therein lies your network. How would you plot them in accordance with the following graph?

Your Physical Network and Your Virtual Network

One additional factor which should be taken into consideration in the cultivation of your network is the enormous power of technology. Think about your colleagues, bosses and mentors that are within your community and within your physical reach.

Now think about the contacts you have on LinkedIn, on Facebook, and all the other social apps you participate in. You just multiplied your connections exponentially.

Your physical connections know you best, without question. They know your performance, your style, your strengths and your weaknesses. Your virtual network may know you as intimately, but in this virtual world in which we now live and work, they can be just as powerful in vouching for you, supporting you and championing your cause, and can more than quadruple in number.

Know and cultivate those within your organization and community. But realize your network, just like your company's competitor, reach far beyond your physical borders.

It may be impressive to have professional references in your community. But it is far more impressive to have those references from outside your community, but also those from around the country and around the world.

Just like your company, you now reside on a global stage. So should your network.

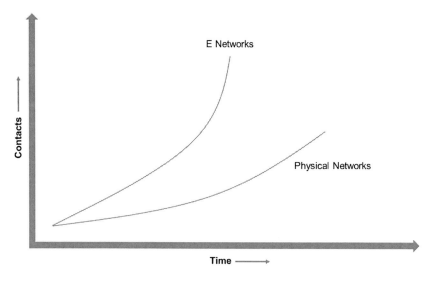

Connect Effect

Networks Are Not Who You Know

Michael Gandolfi was interviewing for a position a major pharmaceutical company. The interviews had gone well, and Michael was asked to provide a list of references. In addition to is traditional list of references including past employers, Michael also included a neighbor of his who worked for the same company. He listed the individual's title as "Marketing Consultant".

During the next round of interviews, Michael was informed that they had conversations with three of his references but made no reference to the individual that work with the company. When Michael asked about the individual, he was told that the employee "was not relevant to the position we're interviewing for."

Michael was told politely that they were only interested in talking to individuals who could speak directly to his performance, and not to his neighborhood relationships.

Networks generally fall into the following categories, those who are willing to help and those who are not willing to help; and, those who are in a position to help and those who are not.

As reflected in the graphic below, make sure you know which of those in your network fall into which category, and work accordingly.

The message is, that you want to sustain a rich and healthy network of individuals but put your energy into those that can provide the biggest payoff . . . those who are willing and influential.

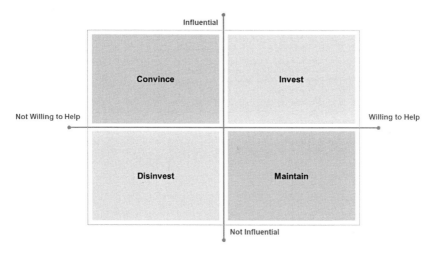

Leveraging Networks

As the illustration suggests, think first about who are in, or not, a position to help you advance your career; and, who is or is not willing or interested in helping. Now, identify those who fall into the upper right-hand quadrant. They are both well positioned and interested. For those, invest heavily.

For those you would place in the upper right-hand quadrant of the previous graph, reach out to them. Let them know what you are working on. Let them know your future plans and if they have any thoughts or ideas of how to further advance. At the same time, ask what you can do for them. Networking is a two-way street. The more you can do for them, the more they will want to do for you. Whether they are your boss, a colleague, or a former colleague, engage them regularly. They are your future.

Now, for those you would *like* to help you with your career . . . but, perhaps have not yet discovered your capabilities or aspirations, or for whatever reason have shown a reluctance to support your career thus far . . . put them in the upper-left hand quadrant of the graph; your job with them is to find a way to let them discover your value. Perhaps, find a way to be of service to *them*. Remember . . . two-way street.

For those who may fall into the lower right-hand quadrant, i.e., eager to help but not currently in a position to do so, nurture those as well. Chances are they will not always be in their current position. We all know of circumstances where a subordinate became the boss and vice versa. Again, explore how you can be of service to them in their career. They may someday be able to reciprocate.

Finally, to the lower left-hand quadrant. We have all encountered that individual . . . The one who is neither well positioned nor interested in your career. Perhaps, they are consumed with their own interests. Or, perhaps, they never learned the value of helping others. The message is not to disassociate yourself from them necessarily, but certainly do not invest your valuable time and energy in them, thinking they will help you advance your career.

With that framework as your foundation to cultivating your network, let us now explore some of its finer intricacies.

Choose Wisely

Cultivating a trusted network is, without question, an investment in your time and energy. Do so intently, but wisely. You have many friends and acquaintances, but only a subset of those acquaintances would qualify to serve as part of your trusted network. These are just a few of the questions to consider in cultivating your network:

- *Do they know your work history?*
- *Are they, themselves connected to a wider network?*
- *Are they knowledgeable about industry trends?*
- *Would they vouch for your integrity?*
- *Do they have influence in hiring or promotion decisions?*
- *Would you consider them a trusted advisor?*

Your network is more than just a list of people you ask to serve as a reference for a prospective job opportunity. Your network should be considered your own private Board of Advisors. They are the currency of your career.

Essential Tools of Networking

When we think of tools, we generally think about technology based social media applications, such as Facebook, LinkedIn, email, and texting, etc. Those are indeed vital tools in the art of cultivating your network, but they are only a portion. Events and activities are equally valuable tools.

Ted Lieu managed a series of technology related projects for his manufacturing company. His wife had an equally challenging position as the director of marketing for a local bank. She had an upcoming social gathering to celebrate a pending merger with another financial institution. Ted was not excited about going to the event but knew he would be expected to go to support his wife.

Once there, he struck up a conversation with the director of IT from the incoming bank. As it turned out, the merged institutions would encounter some of the same challenges and technologies of which Ted was responsible for in his current position. The IT director invited Ted to lunch to continue their discussion.

The lunch meeting turned into a proposition for Ted to consider overseeing the multiple IT projects that would result from the merger. Ted was not looking for new opportunities, nor was he eager to leave his existing situation. However, the social gathering, which led to a lunch discussion, was the catalyst for an expanded network and a new potential career opportunity.

Every luncheon, social gathering, industry event, recreational event, and civic clubs, such as meet-up, the Lions Club, Jaycees, Chamber of Commerce, or other activities where career-minded people convene, are a tool in your networking arsenal. Utilize them aggressively, and make your presence felt. Every introduction represents a chance to give your elevator speech and you will never know who will be interested to learn more.

Networks are a collection of sought-after individuals that you seek out to help advance your career, and the serendipitous contacts that come from the least likely sources and when you least expect them. From wherever they come and however they get there, your network is an essential component of your profession and your career.

How Networks Affect Your Performance and Brand.

Your network and your performance on the job create a perfect concentric circle. As your performance grows, so grows your network. Likewise, as your network grows, so grows your performance. The same can be said for your brand.

The ripple effect of one to the other is continuous. Your performance speaks for itself and serves as the foundation for your brand . . . how you are perceived in your company, and in your industry. Your network is the messenger and the promoter.

As the saying goes, everyone loves a winner, and everyone loves promoting and bragging about the winners that they had a hand in cultivating.

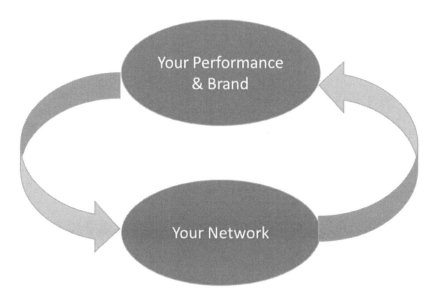

Your Network, Your Performance and Brand

Summary

In *The Emergence of the 'Me' Enterprise*, we wrote that *growing my personal and professional network is the key to growing your brand.* We also wrote:

Networks in a professional environment tend to center around our colleagues, our co-workers, and our bosses. Your continued survival and career development requires you to reach beyond your traditional professional circles. Expand your network to associations, and the global communities that influence your company, your profession, and your job.

That is truer today than when we wrote it three years ago. Your network is your own personal Board of Advisors, your own personal Board of Directors. Just as every successful CEO reaches out to their Board of Directors to lay out the strategies and plans for their company, it is imperative that you do so for yourself.

Use them wisely and aggressively. Ask for their help. Leverage their networks. They are key to where you want to go with your career. Let them do their jobs.

Guiding Principles

1. Networking is your career "net worth."
2. Be Deliberate about Networking.
3. Network with those that know more than you.
4. Mastering E-Networking will pay huge dividends.
5. Be what you expect your Network to be.
6. Cultivate your Network; you cultivate your brand.
7. Get noticed by your Network.
8. Screen your Network periodically.
9. Leverage and be levered.
10. Be Thankful.

CHAPTER 6
InQ—Industry Quotient

THE THIRD PILLAR in our House of Lifetime Employability is how well you know the landscape in which you are employed. If you work in a bank, how well do you know the banking business? How well do you understand how it makes money? How it loses money . . . its risks? Its competitors? The regulations that governs its day-to-day activities?

The third Pillar is about your industry knowledge. It's not as easy as it once was.

Introduction

There was a time not too long ago when an industry was an industry. A bank was a bank that resided in the financial industry. A builder of machines resided in the manufacturing industry. A provider of telephone services resided in the telecom industry. And, producers of movies resided in the media and entertainment industry.

Depending on the markets a company serves, it was important to know these things. The more we understood the industry of our customers, the more we understood our customers and the better we could serve them. That axiom still holds true today, but the industry designations have become all jumbled up. The same holds true for the country in which those companies reside.

General Motors was once a producer of American cars, neatly pigeonholed into the manufacturing or the transportation industry.

Companies were previously characterized in either *vertical* or *horizontal* terms, depending on whether their products or their expertise were in a singular market, such as manufacturing, telecom or banking. Or if their expertise or product sets spanned across multiple industries, such as IT companies who service multiple markets.

The emergence of technology has changed all of that.

Today, GM is no longer just a manufacturer of automobiles, nor is it just American. Many of its automobiles are manufactured and assembled today outside the U.S. and in addition to its manufacturing arm, GM is also in the finance industry. And given the dominant role of electronics in today's automobiles, it is also in the electronics industry . . . the computing industry.

So, which is it? If I want to call on GM as a prospective customer, are they a manufacturer? A finance company? An electronics company? The answer to all of those questions is *yes!* They are any and all.

Is Apple Inc., the company we once knew as a PC giant, now a technology company? Or are they a media company?

Is AT&T, who was historically referred to as "Ma Bell" and known as a producer and provider of telephones, in the Telco industry? Today, they are also in the cable television business. And with the emergence of cellular telephones and the virtual eradication of the traditional landline, they are in the wireless communications business. And with everything from sports programs, to television programs to movies now available through wireless devices, are they in the Telecom business, or are they in the media and entertainment business? Or what? Do they compete with Verizon, Walt Disney, Paramount Pictures, or Comcast Cable?

Again, the answer is *yes.*

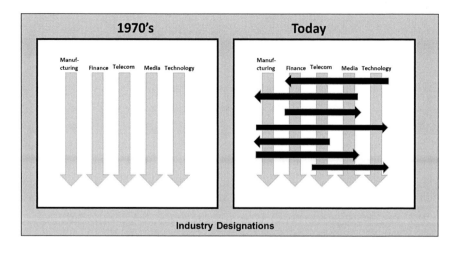

The industries once defined in straightforward terms, vertical or horizontal, are now converging into as mishmash of both. Telephones that were once our lifeline for talking to one another, can now be used to perform functions NASA computer systems could not do during the moon landings. Automobiles that were once maintained by mechanics who were expert in the combustible engine, are now diagnosed and repaired by an electronics engineer. Is Amazon in the retail business? We may think so, but the company's largest profit margins come from its web services business.

Your competency, or your *InQ,* i.e., your understanding of the industry or industries your company serves, is as critical today in sustaining your lifetime employability as much as it was fifty years ago. However, today that is a far more complicated proposition.

Largely due to the extraordinary advances in technology, the industry designations that were once neatly segregated, now cross lines as far as the market, technological and competitive landscapes will allow.

Your Industry Quotient (InQ)

Industry Quotient (InQ): (1) Your understanding of the varying business and the financial models your company; and, those of the companies you serve. (2) Your understanding of how technology is driving companies to create new business models through the integration of traditionally vertical and horizontal markets.

Businesses and their revenue models are becoming more complex. Traditional industry designations are becoming muddied, if not obsolete, as they were once known. Why is this important for you to know?

Well, first of all, knowing the industry in which you work is equivalent to knowing the community in which you live. Where is the bank located? Where are the supermarkets? And drycleaners, doctors, hospitals, and dentists?

So, what's involved in sustaining your *InQ?* The actions today are not much different than they were fifty years ago. If you were an entry-level employee going to work for a company that serviced the manufacturing industry, what would you do?

You would seek training and how manufacturing companies function. You would learn the language of the manufacturing environment. You would learn its processes. You would learn how they make money and what they are doing to improve. You would seek out those who could teach and guide you. You would attend conferences and workshops on the subject.

Those activities would be the same activities you engage in today. The complexities, however, are far greater today.

Instead of a single business or revenue model, companies are seeking multiple revenue streams and employing multiple business models. They are employing multiple processes and multiple technologies. And given the emergence of new competitors and new technologies, companies are shifting their strategic direction.

Accordingly, companies are developing creative ways to help their employees better understand the convergence of multiple, cross functional business models. In addition to traditional training programs and workshops, companies are hosting varying activities, such as cross industry apprenticeships.

"We are employing any means we can find," says the Director of Employee Development for a financial consulting firm, "to help our employees keep up with rapidly changing industry trends."

Consider major corporations such as GE or AT&T. Their strategic directions and business models have completely changed in the past decade. They require new technologies and new skill sets and are engaged in new and creative disruptive thinking.

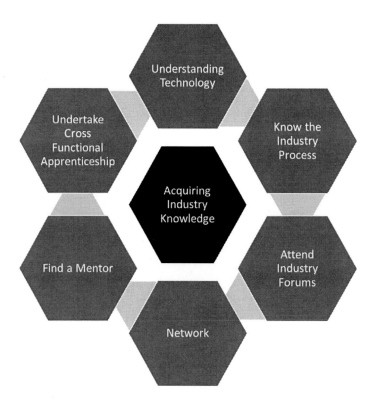

How to increase Industry Knowledge?

Your ability to work and navigate within your industry is no different than having the same ability to navigate within your community. It is essential in conducting business. It is essential to knowing the regulations and guidelines of your industry. And, it is absolutely essential to understanding and effectively engaging your customers.

Raising Your InQ

So, how do you learn about your industry? The answer is no different than how you would learn about your community. You ask questions. You conduct research. You attend townhall meetings. You learn from your neighbors. What are the town ordinances? Where are the best restaurants? Where are the best schools?

The industry (or industries) in which you and your customers reside is your community. To remain viable and employable, this is an essential part of your learning.

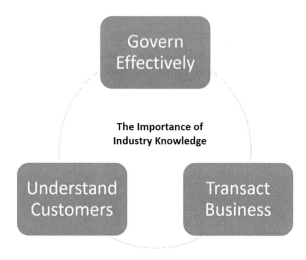

Why is Industry Knowledge Important to You?

In prior generations, acquiring and possessing this industry knowledge was relatively simple. We knew that banks made money, for example, by charging its customers to retain their assets and checking, savings accounts and Money market accounts, etc.; and then using those same assets to make investments and loan those same and other customers money, at a price.

The business models of the financial industry were relatively straightforward, as were its rules and regulations, and its language.

Today, that is not the case. Today, there are new ways that financial institutions make money. The rules and regulations of banking are far more complex; as is the language of banking, including terms like hedge funds and derivatives.

If my job involves doing business with bankers, it is a challenge just to have an intelligent conversation with them. At one time, FDIC was the only acronym people needed to know about the industry. Today, it, like all other industries have more complex business models using a far different language.

How does Citibank, Bank of America, J.P. Morgan, or American Express make money? Is American Express in the banking business, or in the travel business? Or both?

The Connected Economy

Companies, and the industries in which they reside, have entered into a completely new paradigm. Your livelihood is contingent on knowing and being able to speak the language of that paradigm, its business models, its customers, its language, and even its acronyms.

Over the past fifty years, we have watched as companies attempt to transform their businesses from what we know as the manufacturing economy to what is now referred to as the information economy. That transformation has been a major catalyst for the upheaval of traditional industry concepts.

Don't get too comfortable with that paradigm, as it, too, is changing. With the speed of technological innovations, we are moving quickly to the next paradigm, the *connected economy*. That shift, aided by the next generation of technologies such as artificial intelligence and critical thinking, will continue to cause changes and mergings of the traditional industry model.

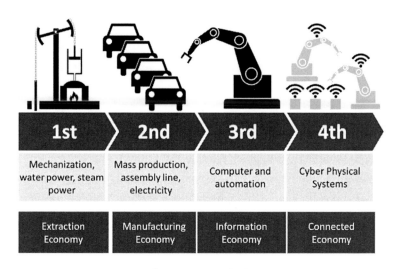

1st	2nd	3rd	4th
Mechanization, water power, steam power	Mass production, assembly line, electricity	Computer and automation	Cyber Physical Systems
Extraction Economy	Manufacturing Economy	Information Economy	Connected Economy

The 4th Industrial Revolution

Follow the Technology

When conducting criminal investigations, especially those of a political or financial nature, the expression has always been, "follow the money." To better understand those changes in industry designations, the phrase is, "follow the technology." Industries today are governed by rules and regulations. They are defined, however, by technology.

Ford Motor Company, by tradition a manufacturer of automobiles, is in the finance business because the company is enabled by technology. AT&T, by tradition a telecom company, has gotten into the media and entertainment industry because they are enabled by technology. Westinghouse, by tradition and electronics, is in the media and broadcasting business because they are able by technology.

Companies are continuously looking for new markets and new revenue streams, and has technology continues to create new innovations, businesses will continue to expand and blur its traditional industry designations.

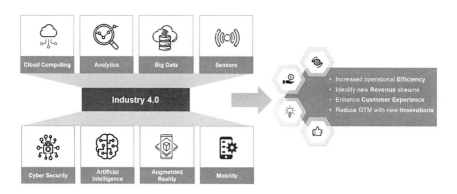

Cyber Physical Systems

We are getting to a point where you could almost throw away those traditional industry designations and say, everybody is the technology business.

What is your *InQ*? Are you struggling to keep up with the rapid changes in your industry? Are you in tune with industry trends in you market and able to engage your customers, speaking to their everchanging needs, in their language?

Or are you ahead of the pack, having unlearned the traditional boundaries and able to point to what is coming next in your industry? Do colleagues or bosses look to you for guidance and insights into the nuances of why GE is no longer the traditional manufacturer it once was, and why it's now a technology company? Or how AT&T is transitioning from being a traditional provider of telecom services, to become a media and entertainment provider.

Where are you on that scale?

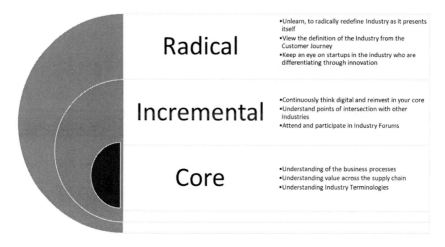

Radical
- Unlearn, to radically redefine Industry as it presents itself
- View the definition of the Industry from the Customer Journey
- Keep an eye on startups in the industry who are differentiating through innovation

Incremental
- Continuously think digital and reinvest in your core
- Understand points of intersection with other Industries
- Attend and participate in Industry Forums

Core
- Understanding of the business processes
- Understanding value across the supply chain
- Understanding Industry Terminologies

Composition of Industry Knowledge

How Your InQ Impacts Your Performance

Van Chambers was an Account Representative for a wireless communications carrier. He was responsible for a series of corporate accounts selling a variety of communications devices as well as voice and data network capacity. With a new fiscal year approaching, he was invited to attend a meeting by his largest client to discuss plans for the upcoming year. He prepared by organizing his usual catalog of products and services with the hopes of securing a significant forecast of sales for his company in the upcoming year.

At the meeting he heard his client's upcoming plans for the year. But the plans seemed to have very little to do with the products and services which had earned him his company's Salesman of the Year honors last year. Instead of hearing plans about wireless devices and communications, he found himself listening to presentations about alternative realities, media royalties, and strategic alliances with companies like Netflix, Warner Brothers and Disney.

For years, this client had yielded significant revenues for Van's company and represented a major portion of his personal income. Now, however, they were presenting a different strategy and speaking in a language he failed to understand. A client that had been his own personal cash cow for years, was now headed in a different direction, with or without his company.

When asked by his boss about the meeting, Van glumly remarked, "It wasn't exactly reassuring. For a company I thought I knew so well, they spoke a language I do not understand!"

Virtually overnight, Van's *InQ* had gone from an eight or a nine on a ten-point scale, down to a three or a four. As new technologies are running rampant in the marketplace, businesses are changing, strategies are changing, competition is changing, and the industry designations that were once neatly defined are no longer. As new industries emerge and old industries morph or dissolve, you and your performance will either survive and thrive as you successfully navigate those changes or suffer accordingly.

How Your InQ Impacts Your Brand

As you have probably noticed, as we discuss each of these quotients, we explore them in terms of how they impact your performance and your brand. Your performance, you may be thinking, is obvious. That is what this book is all about. Your brand, however, may not be quite as obvious.

There is a natural tendency to minimize how others perceive us. As long as I do my job, you may say, the results are all that matter! In part, that is true. But consider, your personal brand is the culmination of all you do and how people perceive you. Your brand is a representation of those results. However, it is so much more than just that.

Think about an individual you worked with five years ago. There is very little you will remember about what he or she did. You will remember, however, how you felt about that individual. Your brand is about what you do, but also how you do it!

It is from that perspective that we examine your brand as it relates to your *InQ*.

Let's begin with your colleagues. Do they perceive you as someone with a high degree of understanding about the industry(s) you serve?

Would they look to you for help or guidance in that regard? Or do they have little or no perception of you as it relates to the IT industry, the food service industry, or whatever amalgam of industries you serve?

The reason this is important is because your *InQ* is a precursor to your promotability, and certainly your lifetime employability.

What about your supervisors? Is your *InQ* brand such that they can trust putting you in front of customers? Or would they be hesitant to do so? Would they engage you in a strategic discussion about how to work with the customers in your industry(s)?

And speaking of customers, what do they think about your *InQ*? Are they confident that you understand their business? Their confidence, their trust, their willingness to engage you and buy from you, is directly contingent on your *InQ*.

Summary

In historical terms, maintain an effective *InQ* was simple and straightforward. A bank was a bank. A telephone company was a telephone company. An automobile manufacturer was a manufacturer. If you served those industries, your *InQ* could be sustained fairly easily.

However, the game has changed.

There are now much greater demands on our industry knowledge or *InQ*. We must know the nuances of how our customer fits within their industry. How is technology reshaping that industry? How is your customer adapting to those changes? Are you up to date on the latest trends of the industry in which your customer resides? What will that industry look like in five years?

That is your *InQ*.

Guiding Principles

1. Understand the various processes and business practices within your organization (ie, how the company makes money; how money flows in and out of the company; what are its revenue and expense models.)

2. Look beyond the current industry linkages to what the next touchpoints could be.

3. Learn the trends and emerging Industry Ecosystems.

4. Look at your company from the outside. Who are your customers? Who are their customers? How do they make money?

5. Learn your customer's journey.

6. Stay abreast of new and emerging start-ups.

CHAPTER 7
DQ—Digital Quotient

A HA . . . WE FINALLY GET to the heart of what has been causing all this upheaval, technology.

In the preceding chapter, we said, "Follow the Technology." That not only applies to increasing your Industry Quotient, it applies to EVERYTHING!

It is not hyperbole to say that advances in technology are accelerating at unprecedented levels and are redefining the way we work and the way we live. By the time a person departs New York to go to a business meeting in London, chances are by the time they arrive, their business could have changed. And only those who can keep up the technologies that are driving those changes will survive and thrive in the workplace of the 21st century.

If there are any absolutes in today's workplace, that is one. As Robert Tercek said in his best seller, *Vaporized*, "If software can change it, it will either be changed or eliminated." He further said, "Technology is here to stay. Your job isn't."

From the creation of cellphones and personal computers to today's voice technologies, robotics and artificial intelligence, the advances that have been made in technology over the past fifty years, will more than quadruple in the next fifty years. With digital platforms in place like Apple, Microsoft, Google and YouTube, innovations and applications that once required dozens of engineers and millions of dollars in seed capital, can now be created in months by a pair of innovative engineers in a garage funded by a Go Fund Me campaign.

The possibilities of new and emerging technologies are endless, and the barriers to entry to create new technologies have been virtually eliminated.

The creation of the internet was once described as the pinnacle in the advancement of technology. In reality, it only serves as a way station to destinations, yet undiscovered and vastly unknown.

Innovations in areas such as educational technology, information technology, nanotechnology, biotechnology, cognitive science, psychotechnology, robotics, and artificial intelligence, are just a few of the segments yet to be fully discovered. The Industrial Age was spawned by creations such as the cotton gin and the steam engine that improved production and transformed the quality of our lives. Today, in the Information Age, technology can weave synthetic cottons and a steam engine can be produced in a garage using 3D printers.

Changes are coming even in the human-oriented services business. Marriott Hotels recently announced it was experimenting with robotics that could take over bartending and salad-making duties on cruise ships and in airports, and that deliver food to hotel guests' rooms.

Other hotels are offering automated check-in via an application or even facial recognition. Alexa-enabled speakers will allow hotel guests to ask for sightseeing tips and order toothbrushes without talking to staff.

Changes that transformed businesses and industries which once took decades to come to fruition, are now happening in months. How does one keep up? How does one stay abreast of the changes in technology and business practices that follow, all at a frenetic pace?

That is the essence of this chapter. Your lifetime employability is in growing measure, governed by your *DQ*, which means staying technologically current and fluent in this era of digital transformation and disruption, both in the workplace and at home.

As one of our co-authors put it, *be technical or be marginalized.*

Technology Defined

At its most elementary level, technology is defined as those innovations, typically related to equipment or machines, and more recently, software that change or improve the status quo, characterized by novelty, fast growth, coherence, and prominent impact.

A few more variations of DQ . . .

When we hear about *innovative* technologies, those are technologies that advance our current levels of thinking and performance, but are eventually surpassed by even newer, innovations.

Emerging technologies are those that are the new and innovative, but not yet fully adapted by the mainstream.

Disruptive technologies are those that change the way we work or the way an industry provides a product or service, thus disrupting the status quo. Uber, or *Uberization,* is generally thought of as a classic example of a disruptive force because of the way it disrupted the transportation industry. Most technologies, by definition, are disruptive in one form or another.

Convergence is when new, innovative and emerging technologies are assimilated into current practices to become recognized and accepted as the new practice.

Collectively, however you define it, technology has taken the concept of *connectedness* from limited to unlimited. It was not too long ago that our ability to connect, with each other, with our devices, or with our businesses, were governed by telephones, email, texts, faxes or pagers. Today, we have the emergence of the *Internet of Things,* where not only we, but our devices can communicate with each other. Our home can connect with our office. Our refrigerator can connect to our automobiles as they drive autonomously.

And this is just the beginning of what we referred to in the previous chapter as the "connected economy".

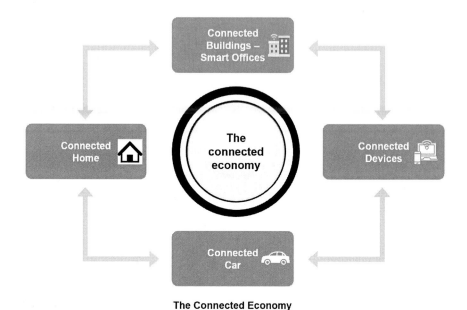

The Connected Economy

So, what does all this mean as it relates to lifetime employability? It means what we said earlier, "be digital or be marginalized". Not knowing the current and emerging trends of technology is the equivalent of not knowing the emergence of automobiles or the telephone in the 19th and early 20th centuries.

Digital Quotient Defined

In simple terms, your Digital Quotient, or *DQ*, is a measure of your knowledge and fluency of new and emerging technologies, and our proficiency in the use of those technologies. The terms, Digital Quotient and Digital Intelligence have the same meaning and are typically used interchangeably.

Definition of Digital Quotient (DQ)—The sum of technical, mental, and social competencies essential to functioning in today's technical environment, and life and in the workplace. It is encapsulated by the formula, **DQ = DD + DC** *(Digital Quotient = Digital Disruption + Digital Capabilities).*

Our *DQ* is an essential component of our ability to sustain our lifetime employability. As technology is inherent in everything we do, staying knowledgeable and proficient in those technologies that are relevant to our work, is as essential as understanding current business practices.

Further, understanding the disruptive nature of those technologies is equally essential. New and disruptive technologies not only eliminate jobs, they eliminate entire industries. At the turn of the 20th century, blacksmiths were essential to the transportation industry. At the turn of the 21st century, employment agencies were essential to all industries. Today, both are virtually extinct.

Chris Dantzler, CEO of a Fortune 500 company, said ten years ago he required a staff of over twenty accountants and more than three weeks to prepare his company's quarterly report. Today, he says, less than ten employees prepare the same report in less than four days; and of the ten, only four of them are accountants.

That is the pace in which technological innovations are replacing employees and entire industries.

Your DQ

So, where do you land in the world of *DQ*? How would you characterize your digital maturity? Think of this the same way you would answer the question about learning a foreign language. If you were an American being given a two-year assignment in Brazil, for example, how would you rate your preparedness or maturity to converse fluently in Portuguese with your colleagues and customers?

For many of us, technology is our foreign language. Whatever your fluency, consider your current level of maturity can be gauged at one of four levels:

- *Level 1—Understand the Need*: You appreciate the need to establish and maintain a proficiency in technology.

- *Level 2—Establish a Presence*: You possess a basic level proficiency in the use of technologies.
- *Level 3—Living Digitally*: You are fluent in the use of various technologies and use them on a consistent basis.
- *Level 4—Leader*: You model and champion the use of technologies, and promote the exploration and pursuit of new and innovative technologies? You are a true *digital native*?

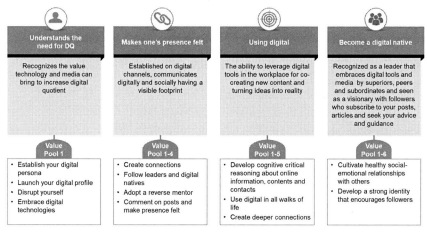

The DQ Framework

Digital natives, like natives of any land or environment, are typically born within the culture in which they live, versus immigrants or transplants. Millennials, for example, who grew up in the culture of technology, are more apt to be digital natives than are us baby boomers. This is not to suggest that baby boomers are not proficient in the use of technology. It simply means that we were not born speaking the language, and therefore must work harder to become proficient.

The DQ Maturity Model (below) can provide a snapshot of where you fit regarding your DQ. From digital native to barely understanding or using technology at home or at work, get aboard the digital train quickly. It is not slowing down, and if anything, it is picking up speed.

However you define yourself based on the levels above or the

Maturity Model below, define your baseline in the language and use of technology, and go from there.

That is your starting point from which to further explore and advance your *DQ*.

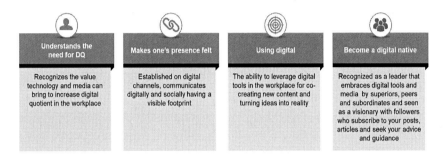

Understands the need for DQ	Makes one's presence felt	Using digital	Become a digital native
Recognizes the value technology and media can bring to increase digital quotient in the workplace	Established on digital channels, communicates digitally and socially having a visible footprint	The ability to leverage digital tools in the workplace for co-creating new content and turning ideas into reality	Recognized as a leader that embraces digital tools and media by superiors, peers and subordinates and seen as a visionary with followers who subscribe to your posts, articles and seek your advice and guidance

DQ Maturity Model

Technology at Home and at Work

Your usage and proficiency of technology can be viewed and measured from two vantage points: (1) your use of technology in your personal life, using such applications as Facebook or Instagram, etc. and (2) your use of technology at work.

Our focus here is obviously your use of technology at work. However, the degree to which you are proficient and comfortable with your technologies at home, provide some indication of your proficiency and DQ at work.

Someone who is uncomfortable with voice technology-based products, such as Siri or Alexa at home, would typically not be fluent with applications such as Salesforce or Trello at work. As we dig a little deeper into your use of technology in the work setting, as we have done in previous chapters, our focus will span the three major areas in which the world of work typically exists:

- *Operational* technologies, such as CRM or project management tools

- *Strategic* technologies, such as planning and risk assessment tools

- Those related to *Governance*, such as auditing or financial calculation, or other oversight tools.

What is Your Digital Competence?

How are you viewed within your organization as it relates to technology? Are you literate? Are you a novice? Do you embrace new technologies? Or, do you yearn for the old ways of doing things . . . the way we used to do it? The answer is to these questions are another indicator of how close or how far you have to go in becoming a digital native, or even digitally proficient.

Digital proficiency can be viewed and assessed from a variety of perspectives. The following value pools serve as a framework from which to assess your DQ.

- *Do you have a digital persona or profile?*—If someone were to look you up on Google, what would they find? What is your digital footprint? Are you visible? Are you known on LinkedIn or on Facebook? Is your profile current?

- *Do you have a presence on multiple digital channels?*—On what digital channels would someone find you? LinkedIn? Facebook? Where would someone find your profile?

- *Are you digitally literate?*—How are you positioned or defined? Are you viewed as a visionary, a technology or industry guru, a subject matter expert? Would I find one of your speeches or white papers on the web?

- *Do you communicate digitally?*—How comfortable are you communicating via technology, such as video conferencing, Skype, or collaboration tools such as WebEx, Trello, etc.?

- *Are you an active digital user?*—Are you being digital? Are you attuned to security protocols?

- *Do you have digital followers?*—The ultimate assessment of your digital proficiency is the degree to which others engage you digitally. Do you have active followers on LinkedIn, Facebook, etc.? Do you get frequent comments on your digital posts?

How would you position yourself on the graphic below?

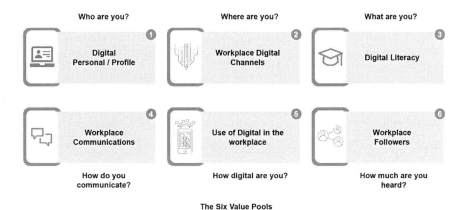

The Six Value Pools

Workplace Apps

The digital revolution of the workplace has evolved from employees relying on large mainframe computers for their data support, to relying on IT Departments, to now each individual serving as their own virtual personal IT shop and managing their own applications.

From scheduling travel arrangements, to planning meetings or conferences, to finding the best restaurant, today's business professional has their own virtual IT shop in the palm of their hand. The applications are endless and manage every activity we once relied on secretaries or administrative assistants to perform.

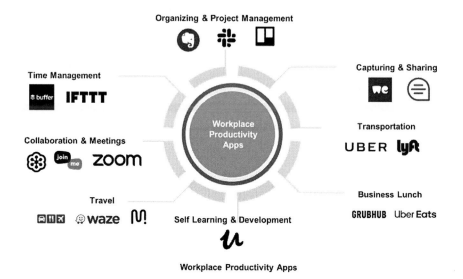

The following is just a small sampling of those applications:

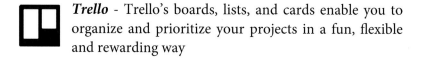

Trello - Trello's boards, lists, and cards enable you to organize and prioritize your projects in a fun, flexible and rewarding way

Buffer - This app for social media administration. Schedule your posts as an alternative? With Buffer you can schedule your posts for Twitter, Fb, LinkedIn, Google+, and Instagram, etc.

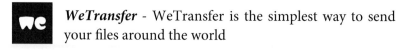

WeTransfer - WeTransfer is the simplest way to send your files around the world

ZOOM *Zoom* - Is a conferencing service using cloud computing that offers a communications software that combines video conferencing, online meetings, chat, and for mobile collaboration.

Slack - Slack brings team communication and collaboration into one place so you can get more work done, whether you belong to a large enterprise or a small business

Evernote - Evernote makes taking screenshots, saving articles, making notes, etc. extremely straightforward. You can even tag and organize them into particular folders

GoToMeeting - is an online meeting and video conferencing tool that lets you connect to anyone and is very mobile friendly and enables easy collaboration

Quip - Quip permits you to create paperwork and collaborate on them with as little distraction as potential, from just about any gadget you can need to work on

 Udemy - Udemy is a global marketplace for learning and development online where one can continuously learn and master new skills

 Lyft - Ride Share app providing cost effective hassle free commuting options

UBER **Uber** - A Ride Share app providing cost effective hassle free commuting options that also integrates food service options

GRUBHUB **GrubHub** - An online and mobile food-ordering company that connects diners with local restaurants making workplace food delivery a breeze

Uber Eats **Uber Eats** - Uber Eats is the easy way to get the food you love delivered to your teams in the workplace

 Expensify - Is a travel and expense application that allows users to manage expense transactions, upload receipts, generate receipts from online sales and automatically create expense reports saving valuable time

 MileIQ - A mileage tracking and logging app that uses automatic mileage tracking to calculate mileage while driving for business purposes

 Join.Me - Instant Online Meetings Made Easy. Quick, Simple & Secure, with a powerful collaboration and a simple interface

IFTTT *IFTTT* (If This Then That) permits you to automate easy processes simply.

☺**waze** *Waze* - Waze is the world's largest community-based traffic and navigation app that can get an accurate time to your meeting destination with real time traffic integration.

To what extent do you use, or are you familiar with, these applications? That is a good test of your DQ. If you are not sure of your fluency in these common workplace apps, you have an immediate action item.

First, you need a primer to get you started. Then, you need to download and learn to use each of them. There are no more travel agencies. There are no more meeting planners. You are it and technology is your partner.

The professional who is committed to the concept of lifetime employability is digitally fluent, both at home and on the job.

What is Your Digital Brand?

These six value pools speak to your digital competence or proficiency, and to your brand. And, both are important. If you are regarded as a digital lightweight, given the levels of automation in today's workplace, it would be easy for colleagues, bosses, or customers to bypass you in search of someone who is more in tune with the latest technologies.

Jack Bowen was considered the #1 salesman in his company. But, when his company adapted Salesforce, which automated the company's entire sales management process, he became a laggard in adapting to the new process and technology. Rather than updating his progress on a daily basis, at the end of each month, he sought the assistance of his secretary to compile his activities on his behalf.

After six months of doing her work and his, she balked at covering for the man she had long supported. Jack was no longer referred to as "Jack the Keen Sales Machine." He was now referred to as "Jack the Drag." He had lost his air of being a leader in his field.

In today's marketplace, technology prevails in every facet of business—be it strategy, operations, or governance. In whichever of those areas you work, it should be the centerpiece of your competence, and the centerpiece of your persona and brand.

Improving Your DQ

The key to improving your digital aptitude begins by improving your digital attitude. Digital natives, those who grew up with the technology and the language that accompanies technology, work and live digitally. They order theater tickets digitally. They purchase groceries digitally. They text, they Facetime, they Skype, they videoconference. They watch movies on their iPads.

They possess a digital persona and a digital attitude.

If your DQ assessment of yourself was less than that, the process of improvement begins by taking on that attitude. In no particular order, consider the following four focus areas as the pathway to improving your DQ:

1—Embrace the World of Change

Technology is moving at lightspeed. With every new technological innovation, our lives change and our workplace changes. It seems we are constantly in catch up mode. From the newest social media app to the newest system of tracking inventory, our world has become a fast moving train that we sometimes wish would slow down.

The reality is the pace of that change is not slowing down. If anything, it is accelerating. So, what do we do?

If we are to distinguish ourselves in the workplace, if we are to try and keep up with the newest technology or the latest app, if we are to position ourselves to have lifetime employability, we must not accept those changes begrudgingly. We must embrace them! Rather than wait for the next app, or the next process improvement, or the next expense reporting software to be introduced, anticipate those changes and welcome them when they arrive.

Today's workplace has become an environment of constant change and the employees and leaders that will survive and thrive in that environment, will have an awareness of the newest trends in technology. They will accept those changes as a matter of course. They will recognize that those changes are the key to remaining competitive in today's marketplace, as well as the key to them being relevant in that marketplace.

If you are not doing so already, read about the newest trends in technology. Talk to your company IT director to learn about the new initiatives they are working on. Become comfortable asking Siri questions or placing orders through the latest technology assistant in your home. If you are not already, make yourself a student of technology. The natives of today's work environment are very fluent in the language of technology. If you are to remain competitive and stand out amongst those natives, you must be as well.

Alternatively, as Canadian business executive, author and consultant, Don Tabscot suggests, if you want to be successful in the future, follow the future generation. Watch what they do. They are the natives of this digital world of which we now find ourselves. They are the ones who navigate technology best.

2—Find Your Starting Point

Being proficient in the language and the use of technology is essential to your competitiveness in the workplace. To be so, the first step is to know your current standing in that world. How did you answer the questions about your current levels of DQ in the earlier part of this chapter? How would you characterize your proficiency today? Are you a guru? Are you comfortable in the realm of technology? Are you a novice? Are you a laggard?

Knowing the answers to those questions are an essential first step in improving and sustaining a high DQ. Establish your DQ baseline. Whatever that might be, that is your starting point from which to formulate your DQ development plan.

3—Take Action and Track your Progress

Once you know your DQ baseline, identify the areas in which you would like to improve. Do you need to become more active in social media? Do you need to become more proficient in your company's technology applications? Do you need to become more active in your company's IT initiatives? Should you volunteer to become a member of your company's IT committee?

Whatever current role you have in your company, be it strategic, operational or in a governance capacity, immerse yourself in the technologies associated with that role, and anticipate what new changes will be coming next.

Get ahead of the curve. Take action and track your progress.

4—Establish Leadership!

The pathway we are proposing is not one that is simply designed to keep your head above water, it is one of how to comfortably swim in those waters and teach others to swim as well. It is one of leadership.

Using the earlier analogy of learning to speak Portuguese, your goal is not to just be able to order your dinner in Portuguese, but to conduct a conversation and lead others, with fluency. What we are proposing, in the spirit of lifetime employability, is to push yourself beyond mere competence, to that of a guru, a thought leader!

That is the highest level of DQ . . . speaking the language and leading with fluency as a technology native.

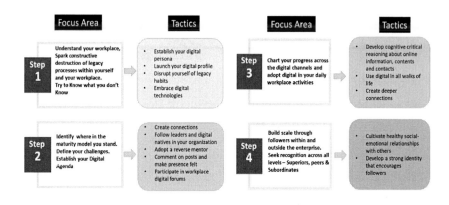

Four Step Approach to improving the DQ

Summary

Technology is as prevalent in today's workplace as is the air we breathe. It is ubiquitous, as are its changes and advancements. What once took months is now accomplished in days. The jobs that were once performed by people are now done by a machine. What is critical to today's workplace will be obsolete in five years. Those who maintain their employability and their leadership, will stay abreast of those changes and be ready. They will stay ahead of the curve. They will remain relevant and essential, no matter the newest trends and innovations. They will be the leaders who will teach others how to leverage those innovations, how to implement them.

They will, as the graph below illustrates, be natives within the world of technology. With their fluency, they will be the leaders others will choose to follow.

What's your DQ?

Guiding Principles

1. There are no barriers to entry when it comes to innovation and use of digital technology.

2. Operational success does not equate to Digital Success, unlearning and disrupting yourself is key.

3. Be open to new business models, as digital disrupts traditional models

4. Learn to adopt fast, fail fast, and move on. Emotional attachment will leave you behind.

5. Keep asking yourself, am I digital? Am I enlarging my digital footprint?

6. Be forward-thinking, understand that digitization in an organization is a requirement, not an option so go with the flow and lead.

PART III
The Roof

With the foundation and pillars firmly entrenched, what is the face you present to others? What is your brand? The third and fourth of the Four P's are Perception and Politics.

CHAPTER 8
SQ—Style Quotient

He wore a suit that looked like it came from the set of The Godfather. His breath smelled of either old alcohol or stale coffee. He spoke in a New Jersey tone that suggested that only he knew what was best. I felt like I was being hustled. I clutched my wallet tightly.

Customer Review

Your foundation and the pillars of your lifetime employability are all about what you know, what you do, how you do it, and who you know. Your roof, which is designed to protect your lifetime employability, is about you!

How you engage others, how you interact, how you communicate is all about you and that begins with your style. Now, let's talk about you!

We all know the expressions . . . *All talk, no action . . . Big hat, no cattle . . . Talks a good game, but doesn't walk the talk.* We know those people. We've worked with them.

We also know the opposite expressions . . . *Would be a good leader if he didn't have to engage people . . . Doesn't know when to stop talking . . . Should be confined to his cubicle . . . Doesn't listen!* We know those people, too. The ones who are all style but no substance, and the ones who have substance but no style. The debates are endless, from the water cooler to business schools . . . Which is more important, style or substance?

As we wrote in our previous book, *Emergence of the 'Me' Enterprise,* they are both equally important! If the goal is lifetime employability, that is not an either/or proposition. It is critical that you know your stuff; but if you want anyone to listen, you must present it in a way that makes people *want* to listen. As chefs from the top restaurants remind us, "The food must be good, but if you want to attract customers, the presentation must be just as good."

If you're not sure what we mean, test yourself with this short, mini-quiz. How do you respond to the following people?

- *The know-it-all?*
- *The one who has an opinion before they even know the issue?*
- *The one who barely acknowledges your existence?*
- *The one who looks like they slept in their clothes?*

- *The one who doesn't know the meaning of the words please or thank you?*

- *The one who's making a presentation with their fly unzipped?*

- *The one who pontificates for three minutes to answer a 'yes' or 'no' question?*

If your answers are the same as most people, you don't respond very positively. In fact, if you're like most, your tendency is to tune them out. Whatever value they may have had to offer was lost in the presentation.

With a combined experience of over one hundred years between the three of us, as executives, advisors and consultants, we know those individuals too . . . we've known plenty of them. Fortunately, they have been a small minority of the leaders, colleagues, and employees we've been privileged to work with, but that small minority is enough to remind us of just how important one's Style Quotient (SQ) really is.

Going hand-in-hand with your Political Quotient, your Style Quotient can be the difference between being listened to or being tuned out. It is the difference between communication and miscommunication. It is the difference between being promoted or being passed over. It is the difference between lifetime employability, or the alternative.

Most of the chapters of this book focus on *what* you should know. Others, like the chapter on Networking Quotient or Political Quotient are about *who* you should know. This chapter, like the chapter on your Emotional Quotient, is about how you engage . . . how you *deliver* what you know.

If you don't get your style quotient right, many people will never discover just how smart you really are. As Dr. Diane Hamilton writes in her book, *It's Not You, It's Your Personality*, "People get hired for what they know. They get fired for how they behave."

Style Quotient defined:

The first reaction many of our readers have when we mention the subject of one's *Style Quotient* is how to dress or how you should wear stylish clothes. How you dress is indeed a component of your style quotient, but it is only a part, and not the way you might think.

> *Style Quotient (n): Your style quotient is a measure of how you present yourself to others, as reflected in your communication, your attire, your grooming, your manners, and your Emotional Intelligence (EQ).*

The Ecosystem of "Style"

At its essence, style is a simple trait . . . you know it when you see it, and you certainly know it when you do not. As in the world of fashion, we seem to instantly know when someone is stylish, or when he or she is not.

To achieve style, however, we need to know and master its component parts . . . the way of communicating; the way we engage others; demonstrating the basics of good manners. Like ballroom dancing, the essence of style appears graceful and effortless. However, the rigor behind that graceful display, until mastered and second nature, must be practiced relentlessly.

How do you communicate? How do you present yourself to bosses, to colleagues, to customers? Does your style match your substance? From the previous chart, in which quadrant would you fit?

Given the following illustration, in which areas are you strong, and in which do you need to improve?

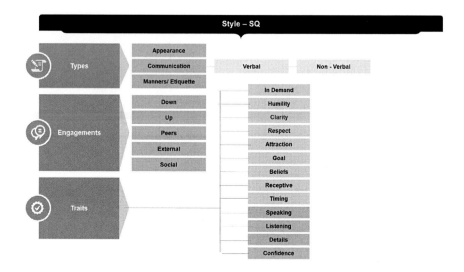

As we discussed at length in our previous book, *The Emergence of the 'Me' Enterprise,* your style, as it relates to the workplace, can be distilled into six major components:

1. *Your Communications*

2. *Your Appearance (Dress)*

3. *Your Personal Grooming*

4. *Your Manners*

5. *How you engage others*

6. *Your Personality Traits*

Let's look at each . . .

1. How You Communicate

Your communications occur in three forms:

- *Verbal Communications*
- *Nonverbal Communications*
- *Written Communications*

. . . and all three reflect your style and how you are judged.

- ### *Your Verbal Communications*

  Your verbal communication is not just what you say, but how you say it. It is a combination of both content and tone. I can say to you, with the tone of a drill sergeant, *Get me the file on the Innotech merger, ASAP!* Or I can say, *Could you please get me the file on the Innotech merger as quickly as possible?*

  Same content but delivered in two completely different tones. Whichever approach you take will either define you as gruff, unpleasant and uncaring; or, as easy to work for, direct and considerate of others.

- ### *Your Nonverbal Communications*

  Just like your tone of voice, your nonverbal communications speak volumes. From your posture, to your eye-contact ("He never looked me in the eye"), to your body positioning, to your handshake, how you present yourself physically conveys a message. Your nonverbal communications either says sympathetic, caring, interested, and concerned; or, disinterested, unconcerned, too busy, or, unimportant.

- ### *Your Written Communications*

  Electronic communication in the 21st century, is what letters, notes and phone conversations were to previous generations. From emails, to text messaging to social media, electronic messaging has become more prevalent, more immediate, less formal, and easier to miscommunicate and misinterpret.

  Incomplete sentences with no punctuation transcribe messages instantly, barking commands and giving instructions. Emoji's now convey what was once complete sentences. Facebook or Twitter posts now communicate our initial reactions, which are invariably poorly timed and ill thought out. Every post, every tweet, every text message, every emoji, and every email, is a statement of who we are and how we are judged.

2. Your Dress/Appearance

What you wear, in the context of your SQ, is not about wearing the most stylish or expensive clothes . . . it is about wearing the appropriate clothes!

Different companies have different dress codes and different cultures. The company that insisted on suit and tie, or women's dress suits every day is today in the minority. Casual Fridays are now standard attire in many companies. The dress codes of the 1970's and 1980's is different from the standards of the 2000's.

The message regarding your attire is twofold: (1) Stay within the boundaries of your company's dress code; and (2) Remember, you are dressing for *work,* not for doing yardwork, or working out in the gym, or for a party.

We all know the man who looks like he is wearing the same shirt every day, or the woman who looks like she's dressed for a cocktail party. And we all know the experience of having not heard what they said for being distracted by what they were wearing.

Your company's dress code may be formal, relaxed or something in-between. Whichever it is, it is still a professional environment.

3. Your Grooming

The message regarding your grooming may be the simplest of them all. Just stay in compliance with the two-pronged guidelines your mother instilled in you as a child . . . *neat and clean.*

Be it your haircut (short or long), your beard (or no beard), your breath, your body odor . . . neat and clean!

Just as we are distracted by any of the above, or even the opposite of the above, such as perfume or cologne, when we notice someone's grooming, it is usually not for good reasons.

Remember what your mother said . . . *neat and clean!*

4. Your Manners

This component can also be traced back to your mother when she reminded you to *mind your manners.* She may have reminded you, "No matter how much you know, you can always be pleasant."

5. How You Engage *(Your EQ)*

The essence of how you engage others is largely embedded in another chapter in this book, and a topic discussed at length in our previous book, *Emotional Intelligence,* or your *EQ.* It is also intertwined in our previous discussion on communications. When Michael Dell, CEO of Dell Computers, asked his employees to describe the characteristics of those leaders that engaged them best, here are the top five responses he received:

- *They asked questions . . .*
- *They listened . . .*
- *They looked me square in the eye . . .*
- *They were interested in what I had to say . . .*
- *They asked my name . . .*

Engaging others effectively is a combination of verbal communications, nonverbal communications and emotional intelligence. Those three characteristics, when skillfully merged together, convey a genuine sense of interest and leave a lasting and positive impact on those you engage and your style.

6. Your Personality Traits

It can be argued that your style is best reflected in your personality. Are you outgoing? Are you engaging? Are you an extrovert or are you an introvert? How would others describe your personality? What are your personality traits?

Psychologist have identified five traits that collectively shape our personality and how we are viewed by others:

- *Openness*
- *Conscientiousness*
- *Neuroticism*
- *Agreeableness*
- *Extraversion.*

Since none of us are psychologists, we will not attempt to turn this book into a treatise on your personality. We will say, however, that your style is shaped by your personality traits, whatever they may be.

As in everything else we have discussed as factors that influence your lifetime employability, be aware of your personality traits and how they impact how your bosses and colleagues perceive you.

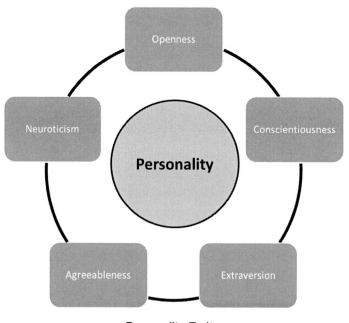

Personality Traits

The Impact of Style on Your Performance

When it came to financial investments, even the major investment firms could not match the record of accomplishment of Walter Lippman, an investment analyst employed by a midsized investment management firm in the Midwest. His company managed financial and retirement funds services for individuals and small companies, and was attempting to win a new, lucrative account.

Lippman was the company's strongest analyst and was featured liberally throughout the company's website and sales literature as its standard of success. After spending over two hours with the new prospect, the prospect informed the CEO of the financial firm that he and his company would be taking their business elsewhere. Disappointed and somewhat surprised the CEO asked why.

The prospect said, "I have no doubt your analyst knows his stuff and could probably even do well for our company. But the whole time we were together, I felt like I was being lectured to. He spent the entire two hours telling me all the stupid mistakes investment firms make, and never once asked about my company or our employees."

The CEO knew Walter's bedside manner was a little lacking but believed his financial knowledge could overtake that shortcoming. He was wrong.

The Impact of Style on Your Brand

Unless you do something in your career that is life altering or dramatic, chances are people will not remember much about what you did. They will, however, remember how you affected them.

Your style is not about being flashy, but about being neat, courteous, and professional in your demeanor.

Which quadrant in the graphic below fits you?

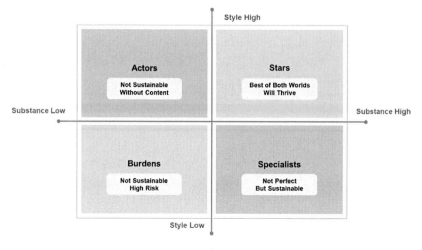

Style Vrs Substance

Gravitas

Those that fit into the upper corner of the right-hand quadrant in the previous graphic are many times described as having *Gravitas,* which is defined as a having a quiet confidence, a certainty or refinement in the way they act and in the way they engage others. That, in the eyes of many business leaders, is the ultimate in personal style.

"Gravitas," one leader told us, "is what I look for in a candidate . . . a confidence without cockiness; a sense of assuredness and not rattled by conflict, confrontation or unexpected surprises. That is my most reliable predictor of a leader."

It is a subjective quality, many leaders tell us, but one that you know when you see it. As Colin Gaudery, a Sales Operations Manager for the SAL Group says:

"My notion of gravitas (and I know there are different views) is that it is the external evidence of a deeply held conviction that the individual is totally competent to do what is expected of them and handle anything that comes their way, without feeling the need to prove themselves."

Summary

Jack Welch, former Chairman and CEO of General Electric, was once asked what he looks for when interviewing a prospective leader. He said:

"I don't hire the man's (or woman's) resume. I don't hire his experience, his college degree, or who he's worked for. I hire the person. I look for the collection of traits that embody the confidence that he or she can get results! And that comes through, not on paper but in how they present themselves."

Your SQ is the measure of who you are and how you present yourself to others. From the way you communicate, to the way you dress, to the way you say please and thank you.

People don't want to know what you think until they know how you make them feel.
—Theodore Roosevelt

Guiding Principles

Your style is the face of your brand. How you present yourself and engage others gives new meaning to the argument, style vs. substance. It is the composite of your substance. It is the composite of your brand.

To maintain and enhance your style, your SQ, keep in mind the following:

1. Perception is a new reality.

2. Style is as important as substance.

3. Invest in Style.

4. Style will enhance your brand.

5. Conquer style—Practice/Practice/Practice.

6. Master story telling.

7. Master articulation.

8. Master confrontation-debates.

9. Be Authentic.

10. Achieve GRAVITAS (Described by others as the ultimate in credibility).

CHAPTER 9
PQ—Political Quotient

I never want to work in an organization that is rife with politics. It is too political!

—*Mark Twain*

I N ADDITION TO how you engage, there is the question of who you engage with and who you do not engage with. Do you travel in the right circles? Do you back the right horse? Can you influence the right people in your company to back you and your ideas?

Yes, we're talking about politics. How you play the politics of your company, whether you like it or not, is essential to your lifetime employability. So, if we're talking about what it takes to survive and thrive in an organization, we have to talk about politics. So, here goes . . .

Politics, like the air we breathe or the networks that enable our phones and computers, are pervasive in any company or organization, or even in any family. Unfortunately, it can also be regarded as being a negative component of those organizations.

In this chapter, we refer to politics not in the context of whom you vote for to be your governor or mayor or president; but in the context of how the natural human instinct of your likes and dislikes align with those that share your values; and how politics can be used effectively in organizations.

Politics, and your *PQ*, is perhaps the most emotionally charged of all the quotients we reference. Some individuals abuse politics, while others are repulsed by the political nature of their organizations. Some companies attempt to minimize their political nature, while others thrive on it. Some people leave companies because of its politics, while others gravitate to it.

Our message is not that you should be overtly political in your organization, but simply to recognize its existence and how it is used to get things done! Whatever the political climate in your organization, do not shy away and do not choose to leave simply because of its existence. Be an astute observer of your company's politics. Unless it is abused, politics is not a personal ploy. It is simply another tool from which to achieve a desired outcome.

Just as there is a political component in the civic organizations you choose to join, or the schools you choose for your children, there is a political element in the company which employs you. Politics also exist, though you may disagree, in your own decision-making. Just as we judge individuals on the virtues of competence, results and past performance, there is also a degree of politics in those judgements.

That's not necessarily a bad thing.

If persons X and Y are equal in their abilities to perform the job, but person Y also has the connections, the interpersonal skills, and a higher level of trust with his or her superiors, which candidate would you choose? Politics as the sole decision-making criteria is bad! However, politics combined with capabilities and interpersonal skills is good!

At its core, however, politics is about power!

It is about the power of persuasion, the power to influence, the power to protect what you've worked for, the power to get things done, and, the power to move people and organizations.

Politics is about the ability to sway others to your way of thinking. Influential leaders are sometimes defined by the *power of their personality*. Roughly translated, that means the power to influence others and get things done.

This chapter is not to propose that you be political for politics sake. It is, however, to say that you should be aware of, sensitive to, and learn to leverage the political environment in which you work and wish to advance. Further, it is to learn how to use your political power in achieving results.

Politics Defined

When you hear of personnel or corporate decisions being regarded as political, the inference is the decision was not merit-based but based on who liked whom the best. You hear terms like brown-nosers or suck-ups, or even gender or racial biases. In this sense, politics gets a bad rap. If politics is the only basis for a decision, it *should* get a bad rap.

In our combined experiences, however, politics has rarely, if ever been the sole criteria for corporate decisions. Politics is a contributing and complimentary factor in every corporate decision. From that perspective, politics is an essential component of lifetime employability. Consider its definition . . .

Politics (n): 1) Recognizing and leveraging the power players within an organization; 2) Favoring and aligning with individuals or positions that you support or advance your cause; 3) Your ability to use your organizational or personal power to exert influence within your organization.

"Politics", says Ceri Roderick, and Occupational Psychologist and Partner at the firm, Pearn Kandola, "is not about being liked but being about being able to deliver."

From our perspective, your *PQ* is the amount of influence you exert, combined with the number of people you can influence, or as the below chart illustrates, "when all else is equal, politics is what tips the scale."

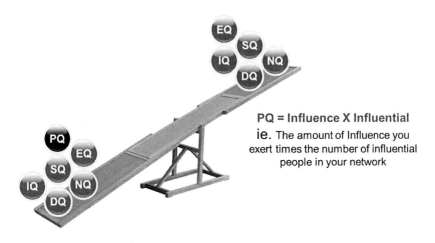

PQ = Influence X Influential
ie. The amount of Influence you exert times the number of influential people in your network

All things being equal ... PQ tilts the scale

The Ecosystem of Workplace Politics

Politics, as one individual described to us, is the "lubricant that oils your organization's internal gears". Continuing, he said, "it can also be viewed as how power gets worked out on a practical, day-to-day basis".

But, as most leaders agree, self-serving political actions can negatively influence social groupings, cooperation, information sharing, and many other organizational functions. The fundamental question is then—is the political power being used to enhance the organization, or the individual?

To understand how to navigate the politics of an organization, one must first understand its infrastructure—its ecosystem. The basic elements that comprise the ecosystem of your company's politics are:

1. *Its Organizational Structure—How is your Company organized?*

2. *Its Environment—What is its culture?*

3. *Its People—Are they highly political, self-serving, apolitical, etc.?*

Collectively, it is those factors that should guide you in how to navigate the political waters of your company. Consider . . .

The organizational structure does not define its political environment, but certainly is a factor. Is it a formal, rigid hierarchical structure or is it less formal, and therefore more prone to being influenced by politics? Is it a matrixed organization, with both a functional boss and a geographic boss? Serving two masters, as many organizations require, means two entirely different sets of politics and twice the players.

How would you describe your environment? Does it adhere to a strict chain of command, or is it more "loosie-goosy" as one manger described? Or is it somewhere in between? Does the environment reward performance with little or no regard for favoritism, or are some players treated differently than others? Lax organizational structures and environment generally translate to a more political environment. Is yours one of those?

And what about the people themselves? Every organization has its share of political players, from yes-men (and women), to cutthroats. Or those that will argue vehemently against the boss' position in private, and then support and praise the boss in public. There are political players in every organization, and we're assuming yours is no different.

It is up to you to know who those players are and their agenda's and be prepared to manage accordingly.

The political infrastructure or ecosystem within your organization should serve as the basis for how you work within the organization and with whom.

In its simplest form, as reflected by the chart below, the political ecosystem of your organization is driven by the following basic elements:

- **The Organizational Structure**—Is it a rigid, top-down organizational structure, keeping a tight rein on the opinions and attempting to minimize any political maneuvering or dissent? Or is it one that allows a greater degree of freedom and leeway in way decisions are made? Is it a matrixed organization, which has individuals reporting to multiple bosses?

  However subtle it may be, the organizational structure plays a significant role in shaping or influencing its politics.

- **The Workplace Environment**—Does the atmosphere or the environment of your organization invite or suppress the political influence of its employees? Is it one that invites multiple ideas as to how to solve an issue? Does it foster competing interest to generate a solution? Is a decision a decision that is final, or are individuals able to influence or change a decision after it is made?

  Just as the organizational structure influences an organizational politics, so does the environment within that structure.

- **The People**—Ultimately, it is its people that shape the politics of an organization. Do the people in your organization actively position themselves to influence a decision or the organization's direction? Or, do they tend to be more compliant, allowing the decision process to play itself out? Are they players or obedient foot soldiers? Do they let the process take its course, or do they try to influence the process?

Do they have their organizations best interests at heart, or is their agenda more focused on their self-interests or their career?

It is the people who will play the largest role in shaping an organization's politics, and on how you respond.

- **Your Strategy and Tactics**—It is your read of those factors that should serve as your guide in the way you play your organization's politics. Whether your organization and its people foster an active political environment, or one that is less political, the key is to find its rhythm in order to shape your own.

The keys are (1) to know your personal agenda, (2) connect with the right players to help you execute that agenda, and, (3) to engage in tactics that are congruent with the organizational environment in which you work.

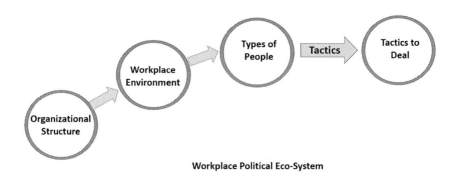

Workplace Political Eco-System

Then, you must judge if the political agenda being played out represent good politics or bad.

The Spectrum of Politics

Let's face it, on one extreme, politics can be brutal. You don't need to look any further than government to see the brutality and dysfunction that politics can wreak on an organization when used improperly. How do you describe your organization, from the continuum of "we only have good politics in our organization", to "it's a toxic, dysfunctional, and overly political environment"?

Wherever your company fits on that spectrum, the keys are to accept politics as an inevitable component of corporations; know where the political power centers are within your organization; and know how to leverage those power centers.

The flow of workplace politics, as referenced in its infrastructure or ecosystem, invariably are intended to flow toward one of two outcomes in support of the organization's goals, objectives or initiatives. Or in support of the interests of a group or an individual within that organization. In addition to knowing the political agendas of your organization and its people, your second objective is to assess the value of those political agendas. Are they good for the company? Or bad for the company?

That should be the basis for knowing if, and how, you want to participate.

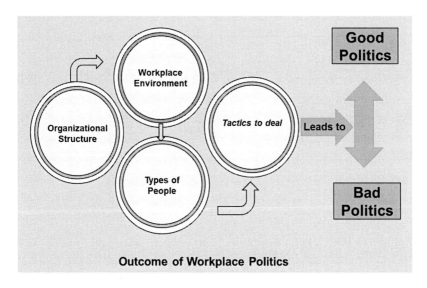

Outcome of Workplace Politics

Let's look at the contrasting nature of organizational politics.

Bad Politics

At the behest of his uncle, who was a major stockholder of the firm, a position was literally created for Rob Pettit in a major electronics corporation. Rob was marginally competent and likeable enough, so the move was generally dismissed by his colleagues as, "that's just how things work."

That attitude of resignation and acceptance, however, turned to uproar and near rebellion when Rob was promoted to a supervisory position after being with the company for less than four months. It was one thing to be given a job, colleagues grumbled; but it was another thing altogether to be *promoted* in such a short period of time!

Rob, nor the District Director that promoted him, could justify the promotion based on merit, seniority or any other type of criteria. Rob, those affiliated with the District concluded, was a political hack. He had friends and relatives in high places, colleagues argued, but not the skills or credentials to justify the move.

District attrition rates began to spike, as morale and productivity plummeted. The District Director who had been strongly urged to give Rob the promotion in the first place, now felt alone and on his own to defend the decision.

Rob Pettit, once regarded as a fairly likeable, but not highly respected colleague, was now a newly-promoted supervisor with a dwindling base of support. In less than a month in his new position, he was ultimately transferred to a different Division. The move, unfortunately, was followed by a reputation of him being a political hack.

It is the Rob Pettit stories in the corporate world that give politics a bad name.

Going from bad to worse, there are organizations that can be so dysfunctional and toxic, they can be harmful to your health, both emotionally and physically. Those are the ones that stretch the boundaries of ethics and even legality. Given the graphic below, if you find yourself working in an organization that exhibits behaviors in anything but the upper right-hand quadrant, you have some decisions to make.

Good Politics

Given all the horror stories we have heard about political organizations, when used properly, it can also be used to achieve positive results for you and your organization.

Take the case of Harry Jameson.

Harry worked as a virtual Chief of Staff for his boss, Thomas LeFleur, who was a Division manager in his company and responsible for overseeing a $2.4 billion business. Harry was responsible for managing other administrative staff, coordinating customer and corporate events, and anything else in support of his boss' agenda. He was bright, competent and dedicated to the success of the Division. He was also well-liked by his peers and customers alike. In addition to his job responsibilities, he was also attending the local university to obtain an M.B.A. degree. Jameson was viewed by his colleagues as a top-notch staffer, but not as a line manager with profit-and-loss (P&L) responsibilities.

When one of LeFleur's Regional Manager Positions became vacant, Jameson raised his hand as an applicant for the job, and surprisingly, he was selected by the interview panel as a finalist. The other two finalists were Assistant Regional Managers, each of whom displayed stronger line P&L experience on their resume.

The final decision would be LeFleur's. When he selected Jameson over the other two candidates, critics decried the decision was being political.

LeFleur, however, had a much more comprehensive rationale for his choice. Jameson, LeFleur argued, had long been grooming himself for the position, plus he was competent, exceptionally loyal, well-liked and well-respected both by customers and by those within the Division. And besides, LeFleur added, who else could he trust more than Jameson?

LeFleur was comfortable with whatever criticisms of politics he was going to encounter for his choice. He was confident he had selected the best candidate.

Lifetime employability is incompatible with an organization that engages in any form of unethical or illegal activities. What you *do not* want is to be complicit with those actions.

Where does your organization fit?

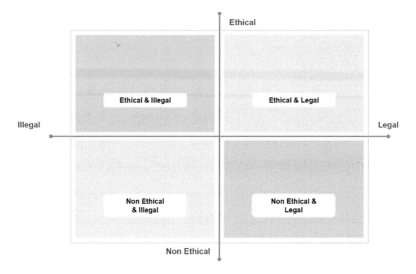

Good & Bad Politics

Success Criteria in a Political Environment

- Ability to influence your peers, superiors and subordinates
- Ability to get things done, while making the other party feel that they were the winners and/or that they did not over compromise
- Think Win-Win - Thinking win-win is an enduring strategy that builds allies and help you win in the long term
- Not reacting instantly and emotionally
- Don't get personal or get angry with people - People tend to remember moments when they were humiliated or insulted, and will let you down when you need their support most
- Networking with the Powerbase, and eventually becoming a part of the powerbase
- Increasingly, organizations are using 360 degree reviews to promote someone, so having an influential base of peers, superiors and subordinates is a critical success factor

A reputation of competence and getting results is the best form of politics.
—Anonymous

A reputation of competence and getting results is the best form of politics.

—Anonymous

How Politics Affects Your Performance

Politics is regarded mostly as a branding issue... *"He's political, 'The decision will be a political one; he plays the political game well."* However, in the flurry of a fast-paced corporate environment, the line that separates your brand from your performance can become blurred.

Kerry Cartwright was unquestionably competent as a marketing designer. Working for a Public Relations firm that conducted promotional campaigns for businesses, Kerry was smart, strategic and creative. He single-handedly designed a campaign for a company, using a highly creative mixture of social media and speaking engagements.

Kerry, also, however, viewed himself as the smartest guy in the room. In previous client meetings, he was known to sometimes contradict and even correct customers in public. Even when he was right, he left his boss, his colleagues and the customer feeling awkward and defensive.

Having already gotten a taste of Kerry's combative style, when it came time to presenting the proposal, the client requested someone other than Kerry to make the presentation. After this scenario was repeated on multiple occasions with multiple clients, Kerry had cultivated a reputation for being smart and creative, but should be kept away from clients.

The natural promotional progression in Kerry's company was to go from Designer to Account Manager. In multiple promotional opportunities, Kerry was consistently passed over for others who were even less creative, but not as combative.

Was the decision not to promote Kerry *political*? And were Kerry's performance issues a function of his performance, or his brand?

While politics may not play a direct role in your performance itself, it plays a major role in determining the opportunities in which you get to perform.

How Politics Affects Your Brand

As the previous scenario indicates, there is often a fine line between performance and brand. Both are necessary to sustain your employ-ability, but neither by themselves, are sufficient. As we've illustrated in previous chapters, the two ingredients go hand-in-hand, especially when it comes to your Political Quotient.

Your brand is defined by how you are perceived. How you are perceived is colored by subjective measures including, your attitude, your opinions, where you live and who you vote for. Of late, the term tribalism has been in vogue. The fact is that tribalism has existed since the beginnings of time.

Accordingly, your brand is a function of politics just as it is a function of your performance. How you manage your politics, goes a long way in shaping your brand. A public "attaboy" from your boss or the company CEO goes a long way in shaping how others perceive you. Your political dynamics and brand change accordingly. You are viewed by others in a more positive light and cultivate the brand of being politically connected.

The inverse of that is equally true. Notice how others tend to shy away from an individual when they have been publicly chastised by their boss or CEO. Their political brand takes a hit accordingly.

In other situations, an individual's brand can take a hit without them even knowing it. A questionable or negative comment made by that same boss or CEO in a private meeting about that individual can cause irreparable damage. Unless that individual is connected they may never know why they were passed over for a promotion, or worse, placed on a layoff list.

Consider the individual's you regard to be effective employees or leaders within your organization. Chances are you would also describe them as being good politicians. Those two characteristics tend to go hand-in-hand.

It is never a bad thing if your brand includes being known as a good politician.

Enhancing Your Political Quotient

One of the most paradoxical principles of leadership is a concept called "followership". In simple terms, followership is about being a good and loyal employee and helping make your leader successful. Good leaders need good followers. And good followers become good leaders. From leaders, to subordinates, to your peers and those that you look to for guidance, politics is an essential element of your success.

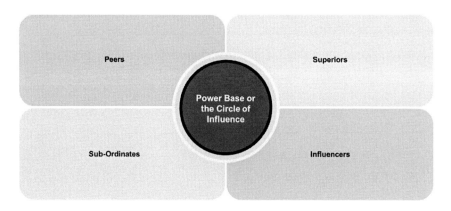

Mapping the Workplace Organization

Followership is not only about making your leader successful; it is also about enhancing your position in the organization. Followership is good politics.

Followership is only one means of improving your positioning in the organization. Consider these basics to enhance your *PQ*:

1. Analyze the organization and Map its power players.

- *Who are the real influencers? (Don't be confused by titles)*
- *Who has authority but tends not to exercise it?*
- *Who is respected?*
- *Who champions or mentors others?*
- *Who is the brains behind the business?*

2. Learn the informal network

- *Who is talking to whom?*
- *Who are the players from their previous positions?*

- *Learn who to avoid.*
- *Follow the influencers.*

3. Build your connections.

- *We began to expand your network across organizational lines.*
- *Do not restrict yourself to certain titles or positions.*
- *Do not be afraid of powerful individuals.*
- *Engage them.*

4. Make yourself visible

- *Volunteer for significant events or milestones.*
- *Be available to help influencers succeed.*
- *Employ the concept of Followership.*

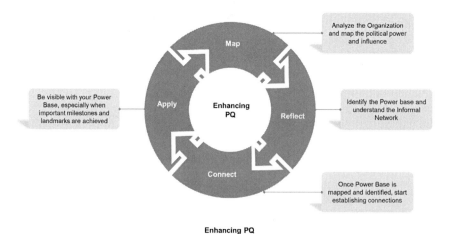

Enhancing PQ

Summary

Politics is a reality in organizations, and not for the bad reasons it typically gets. The difference between "good" politics and "bad" politics is when politics is a complimentary factor in making a decision, versus being the sole criteria in making a decision; or, whether the politics is to enhance the organization or the individual.

Politics is also a reflection of organizational power. Getting things done in organizations means influencing others. Influencing others requires politics: the politics of persuasion and the politics of connections.

In any hiring or promotion decision, when the candidates are equals in all other factors, politics will be the deciding factor. In short, which candidate is considered to be:

- *Well-connected.*

- *Highly regarded by colleagues and customers.*

- *Supportive of the mission.*

- *Has influence over others.*

Each of those traits can be considered political in nature. If you don't have them, get them. Your lifetime employability depends on it.

Another former CEO offered the following simple test to examine the nature of your organizational politics:

1. *Is the activity legal and ethical?*

2. *Does the activity achieve positive results for the company?*

3. *Is that activity designed to enhance the organization; or an individual within the organization?*

4. *Other than the result of creating 'winners' and 'losers', does the action inflict some form of damage to individuals?*

With these, coupled with the below Guiding Principles as your guide, be in tune with the politics in your organization; learn where the power centers are, and, leverage them to the advancement of your organizational objectives, and your lifetime employability.

Guiding Principles

Your politics, like your brand, should be viewed in a positive, constructive light which enables you to produce. To enhance your PQ, keep the following in mind:

1. *Stay aware of your organization's powerbase, quietly and discreetly*

2. *Identify the key influencers in the organization build your connections with them and their followers.*

3. *Keep your emotions in check.*

4. *Maintain your visibility inside and outside the organization's power base.*

5. *Keep expanding your Circle of Influence.*

CHAPTER 10

MQ—Marketing Quotient: Your Brand

How valuable is your value if you're the only one who knows your value?

THE CULMINATION OF each the quotients we've addressed in this book is the essence of your brand—the amalgamation of your principles, your values, your capabilities, and how you engage others. A brand, just as with corporations, is the sum total of how you are perceived by others. A company's brand begins with the way it markets or promotes itself, and then is left to the principles of that company to execute consistently in accordance with that brand.

Hence, the top of the pyramid of what you do and how you do it to sustain your lifetime employability, is how you promote and present yourself, to your colleagues, your bosses, and your customers. Your brand. That can be found in your Marketing Quotient, or your *MQ*. It is here that we will discuss how you take everything that you are, and ensure it is communicated, promoted, and yes, marketed.

In most circumstances, the word "marketing" is associated with the activities a company employs to promote its products, services, image, or its brand. The company's marketing group is responsible for designing and executing campaigns to generate new customers or to promote the company's brand. Whatever marketing activities they employ, the ultimate goal is to make the customer more inclined to buy what the company is selling.

In the context of this chapter, marketing is not about a company's promotional activities; but on yours it is about how you market yourself in the pursuit of your lifetime employability.

In our previous book, *The Emergence of the 'Me' Enterprise*, we wrote at length about the need for individuals to view themselves as their own enterprise; and market themselves accordingly. As individuals, we wrote, we should engage in the same types of activities for ourselves that a company typically employs to promote and market itself.

Marketing and Promoting . . . Investing in your Brand

Throughout this chapter, we will be using the words "marketing" and "promoting" interchangeably. To market is to promote; and to promote is to market. Both activities are essentially one in the same and have the same basic objective; to encourage companies or individuals to want what you have to offer.

Further, as we discussed in the *'Me' Enterprise*, we will be using the term investing. Just as companies invest a portion of their proceeds in conducting research and development and marketing activities, so should you.

Promoting oneself is not a transactional activity, to be employed only when one is in search of a job or a promotion. Just as companies advertise and promote their products or services, marketing yourself is an ongoing activity.

As the work environment has become more virtual and more transient over the past decade, promoting your accomplishments and your value has become more important than ever. If your boss and your colleagues are in the same building or working right down the hall from you, your work activity and achievements are readily visible for all to see. If you are working home, however, or your boss resides in another city or another country, your accomplishments may not be as evident. Making your value known to others, in today's virtual and transient world, becomes more complicated and more essential to your lifetime employability.

The Right Message and the Wrong Message

The phrase "self-promotion" typically congers up a negative connotation. And in many cases, that interpretation is warranted. In this era of "look at me" or marketing campaigns that overhype their product or service, it is easy to perceive the idea of promoting oneself to be self-serving, arrogant, or even braggadocios.

Many CEO's and executives have been accused by their critics of being more interested in promoting themselves than promoting their company. That is not the type of self-promotion we are proposing here. The "look at me" phenomenon is typically about *telling*. The marketing and promotion activity we're describing, in contrast, is about *demonstrating* you value, and allowing others to discover it.

Promotion versus Self-Promotion

In marketing, promotion refers to any type of communication used to persuade. The aim being to increase awareness, create interest, generate sales or create brand loyalty.

Self-promotion is defined as the act or practice of promoting one's own interests, or profile, etc. For the purpose of this discussion, self-promotion is intended to achieve the same purpose as an organization's promotional efforts but avoiding any type of "look at me" activities. That is done by *demonstrating* your value, as opposed to *telling* about your value.

Done the right way, self-promotability leads to *promotability!*

Marketing Quotient

Marketing Quotient (n): The measure of how vigorously you tout your accomplishments or engage in activities to promote yourself, through writings, presentations, speeches, or other activities, all without appearing self-serving or self-centered.

In simple terms, promoting your value is about creating a brand. As simple as that may seem, however, it is a multipronged, multifaceted endeavor. Consider the following scenario.

Imagine the entirety of your activities, from the time you walk out the door in the morning to the time you go to bed at night being videotaped for all the world to see. Now, imagine every conversation, every phone call, every conference call you engage in being available to the world. Likewise, every email, every text, and every piece of correspondence being available for scrutiny.

Lastly, consider who would have access to that data: your boss, your colleagues, prospective employers, your family, your friends, neighbors and casual acquaintances.

As preposterous as that scenario might seem, consider that the total of that information to be your brand. Now what do you want that brand to convey? How would you shape it? What activities do you engage in? What's your strategy?

To consider how you might construct a marketing or promotion strategy, let's begin by looking at it the way we look at each of these quotients by breaking it down as a social or process engineer would do. If you broke the art of branding down to its core components, the what's, the who's, the how's, etc., it might look like the Promotion Value Chain, below.

Marketing and Promotion Value Chain

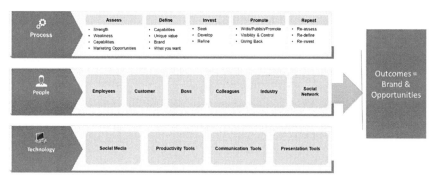

MQ Value Chain

As the graphic suggests, there are three major components that are the overarching components that should serve as the foundation for your promotion campaign. These are the same components companies often use to analyze and structure their activities and organization. We propose the same for you analyzing and defining your marketing activities.

- *Process* (the actions you take)

- *People* (the recipients of your marketing message); and,

- *Technology* (the tools you use to craft and communicate your message).

These are the same three components which are the underpinnings of each of the quotients we view to be the key ingredients to lifetime employability.

Let's take a look.

Process

Process	Assess	Define	Invest	Promote	Repeat
	• Strength	• Capabilities	• Seek	• Write/Publish/Promote	• Re-assess
	• Weakness	• Unique value	• Develop	• Visibility & Control	• Re-define
	• Capabilities	• Brand	• Refine	• Giving Back	• Re-invest
	• Marketing Opportunities	• What you want			

MQ Process

As you know by now, your process comprises the activities you employ to define and execute your marketing campaign. In the context of promoting your value to your own or other companies, consider these elements to be essential to your process:

1. Assess

Before you embark on your campaign to market or promote yourself, you need to know the product you intend to market. Major corporations can spend millions of dollars on analysts, consultants, marketing firms and focus groups to analyze and determine how best present their products. While we don't advocate spending millions of dollars, we do advocate you investing your efforts to learn your true value in the marketplace. Whether you are comfortable with your own self-assessment, choose to engage bosses or colleagues, or engage a professional consultant, your assessment objective should focus on three things: your strengths, your weaknesses, and the marketplace.

Ultimately, you should be able to complete the following statement:

My differentiating value in the marketplace is my ability to: _____
_____.

Knowing your strengths is vital. Knowing your weaknesses is equally important. There are very few superstars in the marketplace that can check each and every box an employer is looking for when considering a successful candidate. Because of that, every career discussion with prospective employers is about strengths *and* weaknesses. It is essential that you know yours, and that you are taking aggressive action to address them. To what extent do you know your weaknesses? And, to what extent are you addressing each of them?

The third element of your assessment is analyzing the marketplace. You may have exceptional strengths in manufacturing, but if manufacturing jobs are giving way to robotics and 3D printing technologies, that might not be your most marketable career path. As technology is impacting every industry at unprecedented levels, are you into with the changes taking place in your existing or desired market?

A two-minute web search will tell you which careers have staying power, and which will be obsolete in twenty years. An assessment of the marketplace has never been more important. Your value is defined not only by the fact that you have viable strengths, but also that you have viable strengths that are sustainable, and in emerging markets.

The end goal in assessing your value, is to know your strengths and weaknesses as they apply to a market or industry that is trending upward.

2. Define

With a clear understanding of where your strengths best fit in a viable market, you are ready to define who you are and the value you bring to your current or prospective organization. You know your strengths; you know areas of weakness and how you intend to attack them. That is your basis from which to define and market yourself.

How do you define your value to your boss, your colleagues or a prospective employer? How do you create a concise message that captures your value and can explain . . . in thirty seconds or less? The acid test in being able to convey your value to an organization is your ability to do so in a concise and brief statement.

Marketers refer to that as an "elevator pitch". An elevator pitch is a summary of your capabilities which you can recite comfortably if confronted with a prospective boss or employer in an elevator (hence the name). That same elevator pitch is equally critical in a promotion or job interview or any other hiring for promotional encounter. The key is to be able to give your elevator pitch in a formal setting, or in a spontaneous encounter, such as a conference or social gathering.

If you don't have an elevator pitch of that is compelling to a prospective employer, then develop one. That is the foundation of your campaign. Everything else you do, resumes, mailings, speeches or presentations, all emanate from your elevator pitch. Think of your elevator pitch the way movie producers prepare a preview or trailer to entice moviegoers to want to see their production.

The presentation of you and your value, as summarized in your elevator pitch, does not need to include a litany of all your accomplishments. That would border on self-promotion. Instead it just needs to summarize your areas of competence, interest, passions, and how you would differentiate yourself from others. Bottom line, how do you, compared to others, best bring value to your employer.

Consider the following that was overheard recently:

"I have been in the technology field for over ten years now and currently manage our unit focused on cloud technologies and artificial intelligence. I also chair an industry group regarding the Internet of Things, and I am developing a white paper on how to develop and integrate smart appliances."

Does it provide a snapshot of the individual's experience and capabilities? Is it potentially compelling? Does it invite further conversation? Can it be conveyed formally, or informally, in thirty seconds or less? What would your elevator pitch sound like?

As simple as it may seem, that is the foundation of your marketing plan.

3. Invest

While assessing and defining your strengths in the marketplace can be challenging intellectually. Investing can be challenging intellectually, physically, potentially, and financially.

Investing in marketing or promoting yourself should be viewed the same way in which corporations invest in marketing their products or services. Companies typically invest 2% or more of their revenues to promote their products and services. It is believed that you should consider a similar framework for the investments you make to market and promote yourself.

For you, the individual, it is the time, effort and expense of getting your message out into the marketplace. From writing resumes, to making presentations, to speaking at industry gatherings, yours is an investment in your own resources, to make you a known and desirable commodity in the marketplace.

In the 'Me' Enterprise, we wrote extensively about how writing, publishing and presenting is an excellent means of promoting oneself without having the stigma of "look at me". Whether it is writing a book, a technical paper, a newspaper article, a blog, or simply finding opportunities to be quoted, having your name on or associated with a byline, is an essential element in branding.

Writing, also, serves as a springboard to speaking. If you want to increase your odds of getting in front of a live audience to espouse your favorite topic and your expertise write and publish on that topic. Whether it is an article, a blog, a white paper, or a book, writing enhances the prospects of speaking engagements. Your marketability and your professional brand increase exponentially every time you write and publish on a topic, and every time you speak to an audience related to your brand.

Are you prepared to invest in you?

4. Promote

In the context of your Marketing value chain, this the execution phase of your campaign. From volunteering to lead a project, to making speeches at your local Rotary Club, to giving presentations at industry conferences, to writing a blog or a book, this is the phase where your campaign takes flight.

Whatever your activities, and however you perform them, collectively, they are designed to communicate a central theme and set of messages:

- *I am a perpetual student and thought leader in my field.*
- *I engage with others to further my company and my industry.*
- *I get things done.*

To reiterate an earlier theme... your marketing campaign to promote your competence and leadership is *not* a campaign of telling others how great you are. It is a campaign of demonstrating that greatness. It is a campaign of putting yourself in situations that allow your colleagues, bosses and prospective employers discover that greatness.

As a former colleague once said when asked how to get ahead, he responded, "*Promote. Promote. Promote!*"

5. Repeat

As we said at the beginning of this chapter, your efforts to market and promote yourself is a continuous process. In the 1970's, the shelf life of a product's value and usefulness was estimated to be 24-30 months. That was the amount of time that was estimated the product could sustain customer revenues before being overrun by newer and more effective versions. Today, the shelf life value of a product is estimated to be less than six months, before it is overtaken by a newer, better and cheaper alternative.

It can be said that the effective brand of an employee's shelf life is comparable. With changes in technology, market conditions, competitive positioning and skills, the Me Enterprise does not rely on what has worked up to now. Marketing and promoting yourself is an ongoing, iterative process of continually re-assessing the market, re-branding your skills and capabilities to match market conditions, and re-promoting those skills to the market.

Many companies conduct annual, if not quarterly, market assessments for their products and services. What is selling? What is not? How is the marketplace changing? How can we better present ourselves in the marketplace? These are the same types of questions that you should be asking and incorporating into your promotional activities.

Your promotion plan should be able to conclude with the mantra: "I recognize that my market is continually changing, and that I must continually re-examine my skills and my position in the market, and my brand."

People

MQ People

The second dimension of your marketing and promotional campaign is your audience . . . the people you hope to influence. Ironically, the people you want to reach are the same people that will help you spread your message, such as your employees, your customers, colleagues, your bosses, your prospective employees, and those you engage through your social networks.

For better or worse, you have a brand, a reputation.

All of the above audiences that know you, have an opinion of you. They either view you in a positive light, a negative light, or indifferently. Others who don't know you have no opinion at all. Your job is to ensure that all who can potentially impact your career, first, know who you are, and secondly, view you in a most favorable light.

Let's consider each of the following.

• *Employees*

Your employees are a powerful bloc in disseminating your message. Whether you are privy to the conversations or not, you are being voted on every day by your employees. You are being promoted either in a favorable or unfavorable light every day, and the message spreads to every other category of person in this list.

Your employees know your strengths, weaknesses, and how you engage others, better than anyone else in the marketplace. Prospective employers view the opinions of the people that work for you as a major indicator of your effectiveness and potential success in new ventures.

Minimize or discount the power of their voice at your own risk.

• *Customers*

Like your employees, your customers know you at your very best and at your worse. They know if you are reliable or not. They know or, at least, have opinions about your strengths and weaknesses, and are the ultimate barometer of your competence and your success.

Your customers or potential customers should be a primary focus of your marketing and promotion campaign, echoing the themes of your elevator pitch and message. They will also, for better or for worse, be a primary purveyor of that message.

• *Boss*

Your boss has many responsibilities that extend beyond your capabilities and potential. They may have a general knowledge of your strengths and weaknesses, but typically judge you on the answers to two questions: Does he or she do what they say they will do? And, do they deliver the goods? (Back to the Execution Quotient).

They are also notorious for getting feedback on you from others, especially your employees and your customers.

Your boss is results oriented. Those who are not, are not bosses for very long. In the development and promoting of your career, your task with your boss is twofold:

- *Ensure that your boss answers "absolutely" when those two questions are asked of you.*
- *Seek guidance and mentorship from your boss.*

Share your career goals and aspirations with your boss. Share your plans. Seek their feedback. Seek their guidance. Ask them to mentor you.

Your boss is obviously in a powerful position to influence your career. Make them an active participant in the process and make them a fan. Make them *want* to see you succeed.

• *Colleagues*

Our colleagues are our comrades in arms. They perform the same work as us. They enjoy the same rewards. They endure the same challenges. For those reasons, they appreciate our successes more than most others. They know what we had to go through to achieve those successes.

Colleagues can also, however, be competitors, or even worse, detractors. Vying for the same position can certainly present awkward situations. Additionally, colleagues are your closest associates and tend to have the strongest opinions of you, positively or negatively. These are situations where human nature prevails.

If you wish your colleagues to support your success, support theirs.

• *Your Industry*

Your personal brand extends beyond your company. And it should. With the emergence of technologies and global competition, industries are becoming smaller and more intimate. The sales leader in one company knows the sales leaders in competitive companies, and how they are performing. Industry leaders know their competition as much as they know their own companies. Your competitor today could become your employer tomorrow.

Your participation in industry conferences are more than an opportunity to learn . . . they are an opportunity to promote. From participating in committees, to making presentations, to presenting white papers, industry forums provide a powerful means to extend your personal brand.

Beyond conferences, there are other means to make your presence felt as a thought leader in your industry. There are newsletters, online blogs, and other publications that provide some more opportunities.

How you present yourself to your industry colleagues speaks volumes about you and to your perspectives employers.

• *Your Social Network*

If you are typical in today's marketplace, you have a presence on LinkedIn, Facebook, Twitter, as well as other social media outlets. Social media is not only an opportunity to learn and stay connected. It is also a growing means in which to promote. It can also be a means to detract. What you post and how you post messages on your social media accounts go a long way to shape the way your brand, both within your company and your industry.

Jim Caldwell fancied himself to be an expert in project management and actively posted his thoughts and opinions on the subject through his social media accounts. Rather than praise or support other people's comments related to the subject, he felt he could demonstrate his superior expertise by critiquing others. Essentially, his posts could best be characterized as 'one-upsmanship.' If others posted comments that were considered smart, he thought, his comments would be even smarter!

Rather than cultivate a brand of that as an expert, he was viewed as one who simply sat on the sidelines, critiquing others. That is not the brand you want nor is it one your colleagues will appreciate.

Technology

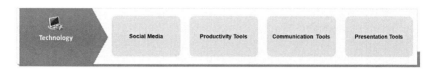

MQ Technology

The third major component of your marketing and promotion campaign is technology, the array of tools you use to execute that campaign. If the process is the what and the people are the who and technology is the how of your campaign.

What are the tools that are essential to the rollout or execution of your campaign? Here are a few.

• *Social Media*

Of all the technologies, the one that is emerging as the most powerful is social media. As addressed in the previous segment, your presence on social media outlets conveys, perhaps, the most prevailing message about your personal and professional brand. For that reason, social media should be considered your most vital tool in your arsenal.

Social media is also a very ubiquitous tool. Everything you post is a reflection of your brand. If you have a personal or political opinion about a topic, keep it to yourself! Another way to sabotage your promotional efforts is by posting personal or controversy will topics on Facebook, LinkedIn, or any other media outlet. Social media is a very powerful tool, for better or for worse.

Keep one cardinal rule in mind as it relates to posting or responding on social media: assume *everyone* will read it and will form an opinion about you. Whether that opinion is positive, constructive, or destructive, is up to you.

• *Productivity Tools*

The degree to which your personal brand is viewed in a favorable light, is largely dependent on your proficiency to produce and project that brand, and your proficiency in the use of those tools. Unless you fall into the rare 3% of leaders who have the luxury of private secretaries, much of your promotional documents are typically produced by you, or at Staples or Office Depot etc., or they don't get done. Whereas leaders and executives were once too busy (or too proud) to learn these basic secretarial tools, in today's marketplace, it is imperative.

From the basic suite of Microsoft Office tools, such as Word, Excel and PowerPoint, or their Apple or Google equivalents, to the more sophisticated voice-to-text, web development and video tools, these have become staples of the workforce and the market.

• *Communication Tools*

In a recent interview for a divisional director's position at a high-tech firm, the schedule that was sent to the attendees, including the following:

'Each candidate will have a maximum of 30 minutes to make their presentations. Please limit your information packets to a maximum of 10 pages. Audio and visual equipment will be available to accommodate PowerPoint presentations and video conferencing. Please communicate your requirements to the scheduling coordinator no later than five days prior to the interview dates. Thank you.'

Remember when a resume and accompanying documentation was all that was expected in an interview, or in an introductory letter? Well, no more. The game has changed, and so must you. Technology has afforded us infinite means of communicating. The burden is ours to use them all.

People, Process and Technology—Your Roadmap

In summary, the combined elements of People, Process, and Technology, as in each of the other quotients we address in achieving lifetime employability, provide a roadmap of how you develop and sustain your marketing quotient (*MQ*).

Who is my audience?

What are the most effective means to reach those audiences? and,

With what tools?

If you answer each of those questions, and act on each of the answers, you are on your way.

A Couple More Considerations . . .

As you use the preceding questions to cultivate your brand and your MQ, there are two other factors to consider along the way . . .

1. Visibly in Control

Not all your activities or your achievements are readily apparent to others. For that reason, we previously wrote about the concept of *Visibly in Control.*

In it, we wrote about the concept of Alpha Dog positions, such as CEO's, Doctors, or Directors, and leaders and how they were highly visible. Their performance is well known to their employer and to their customers. Other positions or responsibilities can have less visibility. In those situations, we further wrote that if you are not in an Alpha Dog position, you have to take extra steps to make your abilities and accomplishments more visible, employing the concept of *Visibly in Control.*

In certain cases, even when your work is absolutely essential to your customer's success, the work you do to sustain that success can be largely invisible, unless you make it so. That is even truer in a virtual work environment, when people are working at home, or working remotely.

A local IT computer maintenance shop in New York City was in the third year of its contract with credit card giant, MasterCard, providing mission critical support to the company's computer operations. When it came time to renew their contract for a fourth year, the shop was notified that the credit card company's internal IT group had conducted an analysis of their work and determined "there was not sufficient evidence of value" for the amount of money they were being paid. As a result, MasterCard planned to reduce the amount of their contract by 40%.

In preparing a response to this potentially devastating action, the leadership team of the IT shop conducted their own analysis of their performance, and in doing so, discovered what they believed was the disconnect in perceived value. They realized that over 90% of their computer maintenance activities were performed overnight, when their customer's employees were home in bed. They further realized that all major upgrades were performed on long, holiday weekends, again, when their customer was away from their desks and largely unaware of the work that was being performed.

They realized they had done a poor job of effectively communicating their activities and performance to their customer. They assumed that their work would be self-evident, thus requiring no significant communications other than their routine project reports. They assumed their work would speak for itself. To the contrary, they realized that their work, and their value to their customer was largely invisible.

The firm decided to launch an aggressive communications campaign they entitled, *Visibly in Control*. They identified which customer was the beneficiary of each project they performed and made it a point to have a telephone or face-to-face conversation with that individual, at every milestone in the project, followed by a mini-celebration at the successful conclusion of each project.

The campaign helped the company renew their contract at its previous levels with no reductions, and they were later recognized by MasterCard as their #1 IT provider.

Is your work *visibly in control?* Are you assuming that the value of your work is self-evident? Are you taking steps to ensure that your value is fully recognized and celebrated by your company? And by your customer!

2. Your Personality

A final note about the people you engage in your promotion campaign . . .

Remain cognizant that, as you define the various colleagues, bosses and customers you hope to engage in your promotions campaign, there is one more thing that will always be front and center in their minds— your personality.

Beyond the training you undergo, the competence you demonstrate, and the vast range of experiences you reflect on your resume, it is your personality that will be at the forefront of all who know you. Your personality will either enhance your campaign, or it will hamper it, and ultimately, your employability.

Does your personality reflect you as having a "me first" attitude? Or, does it reflect you being a team player? Are you perceived as being easy to get along with, or difficult? Would you be described as standoffish, or one who engages comfortably in a crowd?

It has been typically believed by behavioral scientists and others that you cannot change your personality. You are who you are. While that may be generally true, you can certainly make yourself more engaging and pleasant to be with. The quickest way to sabotage your efforts to promote yourself is to project yourself as someone you are not. In that case, you can be branded as inauthentic, a phony. However, you don't have to be rude or offensive in the process.

"Tough, but fair" can be an admirable brand. "Tough, offensive, and hard to take", however, is not.

So, what is your Marketing Quotient?

So, with all of that said, how do you rate? To what extent are your activities and results visible to others, your boss, your colleagues, your customers, or others in your industry? Are you one who actively promotes your brand, or do you assume that your work speaks for itself?

Take the following assessment to see how you rate in terms of your Marketing Quotient. Do you score in the green? Or in the red? Or somewhere in between? The answer should guide you in terms of your actions and the audiences that need to better know and appreciate your value.

Marketing Quotient

Rate yourself in each of the following with 5 being the most, 1 being the least. Total points - 80-100 = Green 60 - 79 = Yellow, Below 60 = Red Needs action
Any individual item rated less then a 3 = Red and means need action

Process

To what extent and how critically do you analyze your:

. Strengths	5	4	3	2	1
. Weaknesses	5	4	3	2	1
. The Marketplace	5	4	3	2	1

To what extent do you have a clear plan to address each?

. Strengths	5	4	3	2	1
. Weaknesses	5	4	3	2	1
. The Marketplace	5	4	3	2	1
To what extent do you plan your time and resources to engage in self-promotional activities?	5	4	3	2	1
To what extent do you actively execute these activities?	5	4	3	2	1
To what extent do you sustain your promotional activities on a continuos basis?	5	4	3	2	1

People

To what extent do you actively engage the following in your promotional activities?

Your Employees	5	4	3	2	1
Your Customers?	5	4	3	2	1
Your Superiors?	5	4	3	2	1
Your Colleagues?	5	4	3	2	1
Your Industry Colleagues and Leaders?	5	4	3	2	1
Your social network (i.e., LinkedIn,Facebook, Instagra, etc.)?	5	4	3	2	1

Technology

To what extent are you proficient and actively use the following in your promotions, campaign?

Social Media?	5	4	3	2	1
ProductivityTools (Microsoft Word, Powerpoint, (Work, Google doc., etc)	5	4	3	2	1
Communication Tools (Emails, Campaigns, etc.)?	5	4	3	2	1
Presentation Tools	5	4	3	2	1
Rate your aggressiveness in engaging in self promotional activities and success in finding new opportunities?	5	4	3	2	1

Total Ranking

What are the areas where you excel at marketing yourself in your company? Or in the Marketplace? And, where do you have remedial work to do?

Whatever your score, consider the work associated with promoting your value to be an essential investment in your lifetime employability.

Enhancing Your Brand and Your Career

Regardless of the score of the above MQ self-assessment, your MQ is always variable and constantly in motion. Organizations change, new people are introduced, you change jobs or companies and, you move higher into the organization.

As you advance in the workplace, you and your brand become more visible. You are exposed to many different situations and more critical audiences. Those situations can become a liability to your brand, or greater opportunities to enhance your brand.

Using the graph below, for example, when you enter an organization, you are measured largely on two things: your substance or productivity and your personality. The major component being your substance.

As you advance in the organization, however, the focus on your personality becomes greater. Your brand which was at one time defined largely by your results, is now defined equally by your personality, your style. The careers of many effective leaders who were experts in their field, have been undermined by their style and the way they interacted with others.

Should you advance to the ranks of senior leadership, there is even more emphasis on your style. Your results still matter as they always have, but your ability to promote yourself as a thought leader or a visionary becomes increasingly important. Writing white papers, giving speeches, or making presentations at industry conferences, become the norm.

As you consider your marketing strategy, factor and these increased expectations and your need to enhance your brand as you advance.

MQ Workplace Emphasis

Summary

So, why is your *MQ* so important? And, why is it more important today than it may have been ten years ago? Or twenty years ago? And, how is this not simply bragging about myself?

First things first . . . .

Your lifetime employability and promotability is contingent on consistently delivering value to your organization and people *recognizing* that you deliver value. The more people know and understand your ability to produce results, and your track record of delivering results, the more valuable you are to your company. And, the more attractive you are to other companies.

Also, the more the workplace is driven by technology, the more virtual we become, and the less visible we become. The more your work environment crosses multiple cities and multiple countries, the less others can know or appreciate our work unless we take extended measures. Hence, the need to make others aware of our value becomes greater.

Finally, making others aware of our value, done the right way, is far from bragging. If I continually talk about myself and how good I am in the workplace, that could be considered bragging. If I engage in writing white papers, making industry presentations, or conducting workshops that enlighten or deliver value, however, I am making myself visible for the world to see.

Promoting is not about *telling*... it is about *doing*! It is about delivering results and making those results evident through those various activities.

When you are more visible, for the right reasons, you are more valuable.

Consider the following Guiding Principles as you assess and work to enhance your Marketing Quotient. Following these guidelines, you will become more visible, more marketable, more promotable, and hence, more employable.

Guiding Principles

To continue to enhance your *MQ,* consider the following . . .
Define and Articulate your value

1. *Define your target audience*

2. *Assert your value proposition*

3. *Actively Engage your Network*

4. *Sense, Intercept and Act on Negative Perceptions*

5. *Pro-Actively Employ Social Media and Technology*

6. *Own your success and make it visible*

7. *Give Back*

8. *Promote Accomplishments of others*

9. *Timing*

PART IV
Taking Action

So, now that you know, what are you going to do about it? Beyond knowing the four P's of lifetime employability, Part IV is intended to illustrate the tools that are available to help you translate that knowledge into action.

CHAPTER 11
The BQS

Knowing without doing equates to not knowing.

—Anonymous

As we preached in the Execution Quotient (Chapter 4), "nothing else matters if you aren't able to execute." In that same spirit, to help you plan and execute your actions to achieve lifetime employability, we want to provide the tools to help you get started on your journey. Part IV of this book outlines those tools and the guidance on how to access each, which are available on our website, www.themeenterprise.com.

The Balanced Quotient Scorecard

The first of those tools is what we call, *The Balanced Quotient Scorecard*, or BQS. The BQS is your means of assessing your strengths and weaknesses within each of the 4P's of Principles, Performance, Perception and Politics, and their quotients, and identify actions to strengthen your identified areas of weakness.

Simply put, the BQS is a framework for increasing quotient levels in order to ensure Lifetime Employability. The BQS helps you examine and map each of your quotients in terms of your employability strengths and vulnerabilities.

If used regularly, this tool can keep track of improvement of your quotient levels and monitor your progress on achieving your stated goal.

The ten quotients described in this book span four varying degrees that impact the risks and sustainability of your lifetime employability. Each degree takes you a little further into the realm of reducing your risk and being more valued, viable, and secure in sustaining your employability. Those four degrees, and the quotients that weigh most heavily on establishing each, are:

- Your **core capabilities** highly driven by the quotients LQ, IQ and EQ that simply put, ensures that you have the basic skills that allows you to earn your paycheck.

- Your **job security** driven largely by the quotients ExQ, NQ and PQ that ensures not only that you are good and needed for the job but also ensures visibility in circles that count. Job security is typically secured by ability to execute and network across the organization and have political connections within the organization.

- Your **resilience** in terms of downturns, layoffs or other forms of company upheaval, setbacks and/or mergers and acquisitions dictated heavily by quotients InQ and DQ; and finally,

- Your ability to shine within your company as a **transformational** player or even be recognized within the company and outside as potential game changer. This is largely influenced by SQ & MQ and define the more transformational ability of the individual to Market oneself and be individually known by one's personal brand.

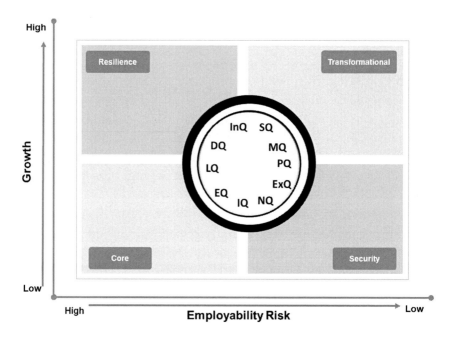

Lifetime Employability Quotient Map

Though, some of those degrees are more reliant on certain quotients than others, consider all to have applicability as you continue to develop your skillset.

The BQS tool provides a systematic means of examining your strengths and weaknesses in each of the quotients and in each of the 4P's of Principles, Performance, Perception and Politics and further, measuring your progress as you go. Consider the BQS to be your self-development and monitoring tool for tracking your success on the road to lifetime employability.

Explanation of the various elements of BQS and Using the BQS Tool

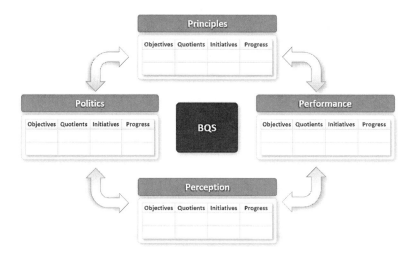

The BQS is designed around each of the 4P's chronicled in this book in terms of:

- **Principles**—How effective are you in adopting and employing the guiding principles laid out in this book?

- **Performance**—How effective is your day-to-day performance as it relates to teaching of the Quotients?

- **Perception**—How well are you perceived by your peers, subordinates, superiors, and customers as it relates to the Quotients?

- **Politics**—How politically astute are you? Are you seen as a player that is engaged with decision makers and influencers? Are you viewed as wielding political power within your organization?

With that assessment, the BQS helps identify specific objectives and actions to improve within each of the Quotients, and monitor your progress as you continue in your efforts, as follows:

Objectives	Quotients	Initiatives	Progress

- **Objectives**—Your specific desired outcome.

- **Quotients**—The areas in which you are targeting for improvement.

- **Initiatives**—The specific actions you are taking to improve.

- **Progress**—A means of tracking your progress on a 30—60—90—180—day timeline.

Using the BQS tool

Let's take some examples of how one goes about using the BQS.

Step 1: State the goal that you would like to accomplish.

Goal Examples:

- Progress to next level in the organization.

- Be recognized as an industry thought leader for a specific area globally.

- Become the voice of expertise when colleagues want to consult in a specific area.

- Be seen alongside with key members of the management.

Step 2: Define the objectives that need to be met in order to meet the goal identified by Step 1.

Let's assume for this example the goal is "to be seen alongside with key members of the management".

Once you define your objectives, you will refer to the quotient map, which will provide you the quotients that you need to target for improvement.

Objective examples:

If your stated goal from Step 1 is to "be seen alongside with key members of the management", then you might set forth the following objectives;

- I need to be seen and heard more in meetings and forums.

- I need to be close to or seen around 2 specific individuals.

- I need to market myself better and have people recognize me as an expert in "Change Management".

Step 3: Identify Quotients that are applicable to each of the objectives in Step 2, that you need to focus for improvement.

Continuing with the previous example:

Stated Goal—"Be seen alongside with key members of the management."

Objectives that needs to be met are:

- I need to be seen and heard more in meetings and forums (NQ).

- I need to be close to or see around 2 specific individuals (PQ).

- I need to market myself better (MQ).

Then, by using the Employability Quotient Map as reproduced once again below, you can see that the quotients that are most relevant to the identified objectives are—PQ, MQ and NQ.

Hence, these are the primary quotients that need to be improved or paid attention too, in order to accomplish the stated goal.

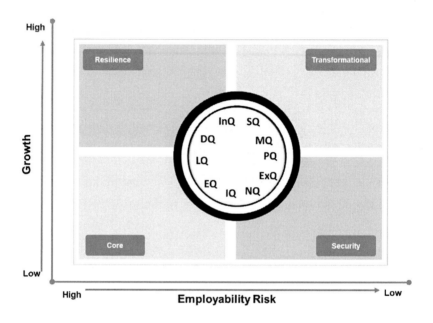

Lifetime Employability Quotient Map

Refer to the chart below, which illustrates the quotient map drawn across the four vectors described above. This chart is plotted with Employability Risk on the X-Axis against Personal Growth on the Y-Axis.

As an example, if your immediate goal is to focus on becoming secure in your present job, you will use the chapters on ExQ, NQ and PQ to improve the related quotients.

Once again, you are reminded that while these quotients identified have greater influence on improving your security in your current employment, the other quotients might still have relevancy and should not be ignored.

Step 4: Create initiatives, programs or activities to improve upon your chosen quotient.

For the discussed example above in order to increase your PQ you will follow the guidelines and principles outlined in the PQ chapter, similarly.

To increase your MQ and NQ, you will follow the ideas put forth in the MQ and NQ chapters to increase your quotient.

Step 5: Measure your Progress.

Start focusing on planned activities and measure yourself both by an external person and self across a 30-60-90-180-day timeline.

The Playbook, which we introduce in the next chapter, illustrates the spiral technique to plot your current quotient levels and the progress across a 30-60-90-180-day timeline.

A sample of the BQS for the above illustrated example is reproduced below.

	Objectives	Quotients	Initiatives	Progress
1	Need to be seen and heard more in meetings and forums	MQ	1. Use Opportunities to define and articulate your value. 2. During Meetings Assert your value proposition 3. Sense, Intercept and Act on Negative Perceptions	Starting Spiral Level = 2 30 day Spiral Level =3
2	I need to be close to or seen around 2 specific individuals	PQ	1. Analyze the organization and Map where the 2 individuals are in the Political heiarchy 2 Make yourself visible to them by volunteering for specific events or milestones	Starting Spiral Level =1 30 day Spiral Level =2
3	I need to market myself better and have people recognize me as an expert in 'Change Management'	NQ	1. Identify your circle of influence and project yourself as a Subject MatterExpert 2. Commment on blogs of your colleagues to increase your visibility 3. Speakout on meetings and forums giving your Point of View (POV)	Starting Spiral Level =1 30 day Spiral Level =2

The complete BQS tool, along with its companion tools and frequently asked questions (FAQ's) can be accessed via our website, via www.themeenterprise.com.

CHAPTER 12
The Playbook

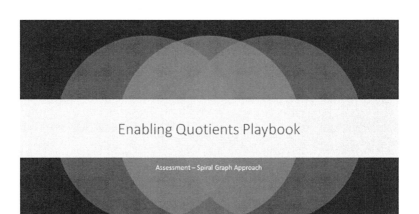

Enabling Quotients Playbook

Assessment – Spiral Graph Approach

THE PREVIOUS CHAPTER introduced the BQS tool, which is designed to identify the Quotients you wish to improve and the goals, objectives and actions you wish to take to improve them. The *Enabling Quotients Playbook* is your long-term planning guide for executing that plan and tracking your progress, accordingly.

Consider The Playbook to be your roadmap to lifetime employability.

Competency Circles

The foundation of your development plan is a basic description of the varying levels of competency as it relates to each of the Quotients. From basic, to intermediate, to advanced, it is essential to understand the definitions in order to first, establish your baseline, and then to track your improvements.

The competency levels are represented by circles, as on a target. The circles, and the concept of spiral plotting, enables you to obtain a 360-degree view of your current levels of performance in each quotient. The competency levels are defined as outlined below:

Circle 1—Recognizing the need—The innermost circle can be equated to a 1 on a five-point scale. You recognize the need but have yet to actively engage in cultivating the competency.

Circle 2—Active—This level represents that the individual is aware and is proactively engaged in activities to develop this quotient.

Circle 3—Lead with confidence—In this level, the individual possesses an adequate level of competency within the respective quotient as reflected in their day-to-day activities in the workplace.

Circle 4—Influence Outcomes—The individual possesses a high level of competency within the Quotient, as characterized by displaying leadership in the area.

Circle 5—Dominate the environment—This represents the highest level of competency, as characterized by the individual's ability to bring change into the environment and influence outcomes.

Using the graph below and definitions of each of the Competency Circles, the objective is to obtain a 360-degree viewpoint of where you currently reside within each competency.

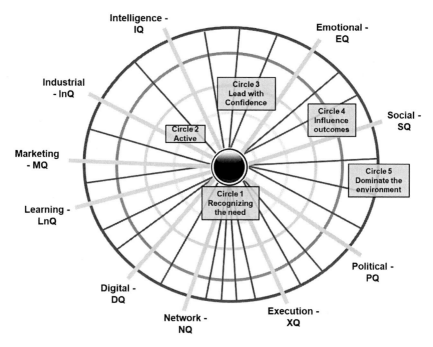

Quotient Spiral Graph – Definition of Circles

For example, if an individual assessed himself as plotted on the graph below, how would you characterize that individual? In what areas is the individual strongest? In what areas is he/she weakest? What actions might be recommended for improvement?

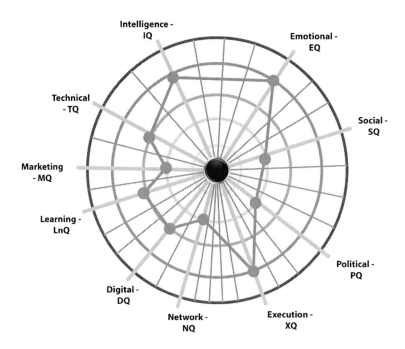

Sample Spider Graph

The intent is to know your level relative to the ten Quotients outlined in this book. Assessing yourself, alone, however, gives you only a partial view, and in many cases, a distorted one. There is an axiom that says, "we view ourselves as we would like to be. Others view us as we are."

It is for that reason, that we propose not only self-assessments, but multiple assessments, from your boss, your colleagues, your subordinates, and even your customers.

It is that 360-degree view that provides a clear sense of where you are, and where you want to be.

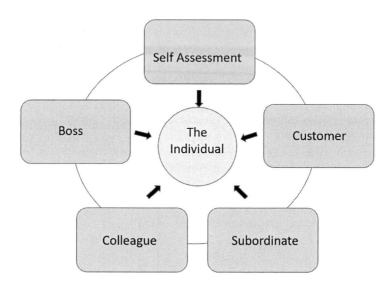

360 Degree Assessment

Your Boss

To take the previous example one step further, what if the same individual asked his boss to provide his or her assessment on the same graph? And, what if it differed (which it most likely would).

And what if the two together looked like this?

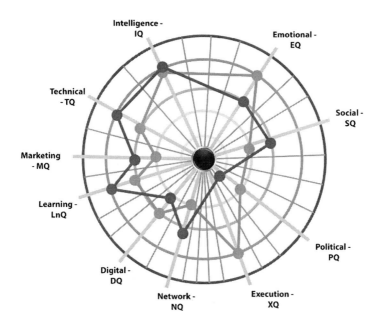

Sample Self-Assessment and Boss

What do you do with that information? There is no right or wrong, but it is crucial to understand how you are viewed by your boss, and why. The actual numbers on the graph are not as important as is that conversation with your boss to get his or her perspective.

Your Colleagues

And what about your colleagues? They observe your performance on a daily basis. They know your competencies. They know your strong suits, and they know your weaknesses. And, chances are, they may even rate you differently than your boss.

And also, like your boss, they will probably have ideas about particular actions you can take to improve in various Quotients.

What if, after getting assessments from different critical players in your work circle, you wound up with a chart that looked like this?

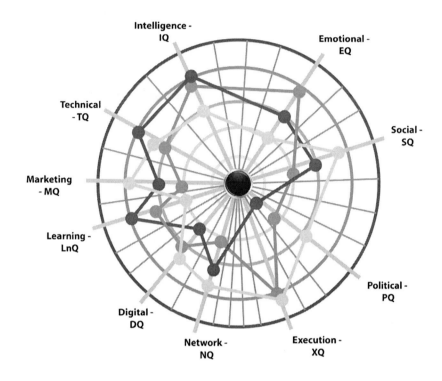

Sample Self-Boss-Colleague

As confusing and confounding as multiple assessments from various individuals may look, that is actually a good thing. Because, behind every assessment lies a valuable conversation. It provides you the opportunity to have the crucial conversations about how you are viewed by those that know you best. That series of assessments and conversations will serve as your baseline and will provide you a point of comparison as you improve within each area.

And, paradoxically, while you might hope that there is consistency in the ratings you receive from others, different viewpoints are a good thing! The more the assessments differ from one another, the more conversation there is to be had, and the more insights as to how to improve.

Each assessment from your co-workers, no matter how different they may be, or how difficult they may be to hear, is a step closer to improvement and a step closer to lifetime employability.

All of that is predicated on what Cheryl Sandburg's colleague asked her after she asked for feedback from a presentation, "do you want me to be nice, or do you want to improve?"

Having defined the assessment framework, including the Competency Circles and the importance of a 360 view, let's examine the process of the Playbook, which consists of 5 basic steps:

Step 1: State Goal/Goals to be achieved
Just as was discussed in the previous chapter on BQS. Just to reiterate, examples of goals could be:

- Progress to Next Level in the organization.

- Be recognized as a leader of my team.

- Become the voice of expertise when colleagues want to consult.

- Ensure I am recognized as a Subject Matter Expert in a specific area.

Step 2: Determine baseline quotient levels across the relevant quotients
Using the Employability Quotient Map described in the previous chapter on BQS, which is once again reproduced here for easy reference, identify your quotient that are relevant for the accomplishment of goals.

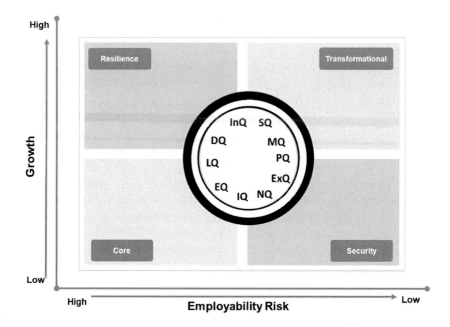

Lifetime Employability Quotient Map

Step 3: Establish your Quotient levels to be attained

Where would you like to be within each of the Quotients? For example, "I wish to move my PQ from Circle 1 to Circle 2."

Use the Spiral Graph Template shown below to plot your current levels, which you can download from our website www.theme enterprise.com.

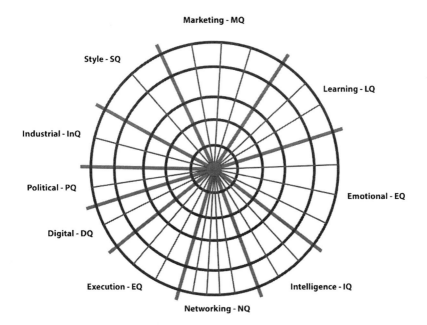

Quotient Spiral Graph - Sample Template

Step 4: Determine your Target Quotient Level
Example, "I wish to move my PQ from Circle 1 to Circle 2."

Step 5: Identify Tactics and Programs
What actions or steps can be taken to improve from Level 1 to Level 2? For example, within your Political Quotient, or PQ, so some of the likely tactics that needs to be adopted could be:

- Identify key individuals you want to engage and develop relationships with.

- Engage in at least one lunch with Key Leader every quarter.

- Volunteer to participate in projects that are of high priority to the CEO or Executive Team.

Step 6: Execute

Within each activity you identify for yourself, or are recommended to by others, identify measurable milestone events that can be used to track your progress towards improvement over a 30-60-90-180-day timeline. Plot your progress on a spiral graph, as shown below. Templates are available on our website at www.themeenterprise.com.

Those milestones are essential measurements of your progress. Additionally, the Playbook provides you with a dashboard from which to view your progress with in each of the Quotients identified as being critical to your lifetime employability.

Together, the BQS and the Playbook combines to provide you the tools and the roadmap to help you convert the learnings from this book into action.

CHAPTER 13
Some Final Thoughts

THE QUOTIENTS WE have cited throughout this book we believe are the linchpins of lifetime employability and career success. There are some additional factors, however that are tangential to that success, but equally critical.

As we reflect on our own careers and those of highly successful business leaders and entrepreneurs, there are some factors that must be managed, for example:

- *Your health*

- *Your career choices, and*

- *Your willingness to accept guidance or advice*

Those elements are embedded in the ten Quotients outlined in the previous chapters, in one form or another. But, given their significance in terms of your career, we felt they deserved special consideration.

Consider these to be critical underlying factors that accompany you as you venture on your journey to lifetime employability.

They are your, *Oh, by the way. Don't forget . . .* messages.

Pay attention to your health

The first of those is obviously your health. Your health is important, but what is even more important is preventive and sustained health. If your employability is going to last for a lifetime, that lifetime must be accompanied by good health.

This is not to lecture you on how you should eat a healthy diet, exercise regularly, get regular check-up's and watch your weight, etc. (all of which you should). Nor is it to ignore the reality that we all experience incidents and accidents at some point in our lives, and we all get sick or suffer traumatic experiences.

It is about your health as it relates to your career. It is about the correlation between good health and a successful career, and how you maintain that. Your work impacts your health in many ways, and likewise your health impacts your work. As such, both are governed by a variety of factors.

As we've cited frequently, the pace of innovation and change in the workplace encourages us, and in some cases, even demands that we now work 60—70—80 hours a week, and on top of that, take our work home with us to do even more. Technology is the driving force of innovation. A downside to that innovation is that it has also given us the capability to do our jobs from anywhere at any time. And unfortunately, we feel compelled to take full advantage.

Who among us has not slept with our iPhones or tablets on our night tables, to capture the thoughts and ideas that are whirling in our heads throughout the night? Who among us has not taken a vacation with our families, and sat on the beach reading emails as our children play? Who among us has not been convinced that the company will run amok, or somebody will take our place while we're away, allowing us to rationalize 24x7 contact with the office?

Who among us has not worked a full week, then gotten on a plane over the weekend to make a Monday morning meeting on the opposite coast, or in another country? Who among us had to be reminded by our spouse of our wedding anniversary, or one of our children's birthdays or graduations?

Weekdays or weekends, workdays or holidays, annual physicals or annual leave, today's culture assumes we are constantly at work, even when we are not at work. Saturday has become the new Friday and Sunday has become the new Monday. The work, the phone calls, and the preparations for the upcoming week or meeting, or business trip never end.

As a result, our health and our families pay the price. When work begins to consume our lives, at the expense of everything else, our health, our families, our work/life balance, and every other facet of our lives suffer.

Poor health, in addition to the physical, financial, and family toll it takes on the individual, impacts the individual's career as well. In addition to the perception issue that the individual may or may not be available, questionable health creates lost opportunity. Every day you are out of work because of illness or a related health issue, is a day of not delivering or demonstrating your value. The answer is not to ignore your health and go to work anyway. The answer is to take care yourself.

In the 19th century, mail carriers that delivered the mail via pony express learned very quickly that their livelihoods depended on taking care of their horses. In the 20th century, we learned we had to maintain our automobiles, by stopping to get gas, change the oil and basic repairs. Our ability to work successfully on a consistent basis is dependent on the maintenance of our health.

The adage, "work smarter, not harder" has never been more critical. Pay attention to your body. It speaks to you, and if you choose not to listen, it speaks louder, invariably in the form of a heart attack, stroke, or some other debilitating illness.

The other adage is equally true, "if you don't have your health, nothing else matters."

• *Your Family*

The natural extension of our health is our family. With work having a way of becoming all-consuming, those that are most important to us feel the result. Just ask the spouse or children of an entrepreneur, a physician, a policeman, or a college or professional football coach.

Whether it is 70 or 80 our work weeks or whether it is reading your email while your child is trying to share something that happened at school that day, we have plenty of distractions that intrude on our work/life balance and our times with our family.

One executive we spoke with described seeing his daughter in her prom gown and described her high school years as being a blur to him, given his obsessive focus on his start-up company. He could not recall a single meaningful moment in her entire high school experience, and now she was on the verge of graduating. He later declared to his board that he would be taking the next three months off to accompany her on her college visits.

As extreme as that circumstance may be, all of us in pursuit of innovation, professional success and lifetime employability are capable of giving less attention to the very source of our sustenance . . . our families.

Again, it is technology that has become both a blessing and a curse. That, which fuels innovation can completely blur the line between work and family.

Pay attention to your family. Find and retain your work/life balance.

• *Your Spiritual Health*

Your spiritual health is not necessarily your religious health. Be you a Christian, Buddhist, Muslim, Hindu, Jewish or other, your spiritual health is about whatever enables you to be at one with the universe.

Our purpose is not to preach to you about religion, nor is it to proselytize about a greater good. It is simply to say there is a spiritual element inside each of us, and as food nourishes our bodies, our spiritual health nourishes our souls.

Find and sustain whatever source provides that sense of guidance and inner peace.

Your lifetime employability and your life will be enhanced accordingly.

Our spiritual health is the pathway to our emotional intelligence (our EQ), which in turn, is our foundation for enduring difficult situations more effectively.

Whether it is organized religion, participating in a séance, transcendental meditation, or some other means, find your source of spiritual wellness and engage it regularly.

Like your physical health, if you don't have that sense of inner peacefulness, everything else becomes skewed.

• *Your Financial Health*

Financial prosperity is a driving force for many of us. For some, it is *the* driving force. And no other factor leads to poor decision-making than being financially troubled. Money is invariably a factor in making career decisions. But, when it is *the* factor, careers invariably go awry.

However significant or insignificant the role financial prosperity plays in your life; we leave that up to you. But realize that the pursuit of financial prosperity is *not* the same as the pursuit of financial health.

The pursuit of prosperity is about the pursuit of money. The pursuit of financial health is the pursuit of tranquility. It is about balance. Balance between prosperity and contentment. Balance between what comes in, and what goes out. From numerous studies, our own careers, and others we have studied, we know three things:

- *If you're living beyond your means and worried about paying your bills or the financial debt you've incurred, you're not thinking about your job.*

- *And, if you're not thinking about your job, your value diminishes.*

- *Financial imbalance leads to poor career choices.*

Manage your finances just as you would manage your health and your family.

So, about your career choices . . .

If you are fortunate, you are working in a company that is financially healthy, has good leadership, and a culture that supports personal and professional growth. If you're experiencing less than that, or considering looking elsewhere, the tendency is to look elsewhere. In doing so, remember this Golden Rule:

Every new opportunity that offers greener pastures or more money, also has a downside. Your job is to find that downside and look before you leap.

To take that one step further, we would contend that any job you pursue because of greener pastures or more money warrants careful consideration before you jump on it, and ask yourself this simple question: "am I going to something, or am I getting away from something?"

If the answer is the latter, ask yourself these follow-up questions:

1. *Can the issue be resolved?*

2. *Is the issue permanent or temporary?*

Any job changes to get away from something usually does not turn out well. There is typically too much focus on the getting away part, and not enough on the going to part.

Also, when it comes to making career choices, consider your industry. For profit companies are very different from non-profits. The telecom environment is very different from public agencies. A good project manager in the manufacturing industry may not be a good project manager in a financial institution. Different cultures, different regulations and even different expectations have derailed the promising careers of otherwise competent, but unsuspecting professionals.

Additionally, consider the health of an industry. An advertising executive from the fashion industry was hired by a major newspaper to revive their sagging advertising sales. Less than a year into his new job, he learned the paper would be undergoing massive lay-off's due to the rise of online publications.

Industries, like companies are in a perpetual state of emerging, or declining.

Choose wisely.

So, with these added tidbits, what should guide your career decision making? Consider the following:

Seek successful companies and bosses

Darrel Reavis was considered the best defensive back in the National Football League. As a free agent, he had offers to play with any team in the league. When asked why he signed with the New England Patriots for far less money than other teams had offered, he replied, "because it gave me the opportunity to play for the best coach and the best team in the league."

You may or may not have the opportunity to work for "the best in the league", like an Elon Musk or a Steve Jobs, but winning coaches and organizations and winning cultures can be found in any industry and in any community. When exploring career opportunities, find companies with a history of success, as well as leaders.

Seek a Culture of Radical Candor

A critical element of a winning culture is open communication: from open praise, to open challenges, to open disagreements and criticisms.

We are reminded of the story of Cheryl Sandburg, COO of Facebook, making a presentation and at the conclusion, walking out with her Chief of Staff. Feeling good about her presentation, she looked at her Chief of Staff and said knowingly, "I think that went pretty well, don't you?" Instead of getting the answer she had assumed, the underling instead pointed out what he considered to be several flaws in his boss's delivery.

Instead of complementing his boss, he felt comfortable to offer her constructive and candid feedback. He felt comfortable because he knew his boss preferred constructive criticism rather than the all too common, flowery, meaningless flattery.

Theirs's was a relationship and a culture of radical candor, which is driven by the simple question, "do you want to be flattered, or do you want to get better?"

Remember, some jobs are better than others

Let's face it, there are those jobs that are at the core of a company's mission, and there are the jobs that support those at the core of the mission. There are line jobs, and there are staff jobs. There are the sexy jobs and there are unsexy ones. There are jobs that get all the attention, and those that are hidden in the back offices. There are the jobs that generate revenue, and there are those that are considered part of the cost of doing business.

The adage is, "the most important jobs are those closest to where the revenues come in the door or go out the door."

Whatever your job may be, look for opportunities that are customer or externally focused, as opposed to doing purely internally focused work. Even if you're in an administrative staff position buried deep in the bowels of your organization, seek ways to provide that support to line positions or organizations.

Companies will always need administrative support and staff positions. But the closer you are to externally focused and revenue generating activity, the more your lifetime employability is enhanced.

Beware of Catch 22

Throughout the entirety of this book, we have preached the virtues of developing, promoting, and executing your value in the workplace. That, as we have outlined, is the essence of lifetime employability. Now, here is the paradox of lifetime employability.

To prove your value, there is a natural tendency to take on more and more work. The most zealous employees' common response is, "I don't know what the question is, but the answer is yes! I can do it." We take on more. We do more. We continually set the bar higher. Even if it takes all night and all weekend to deliver. That is what life is all about in the world of work that is fast-paced, global, and technology driven.

The paradox is, the more we do, the more is expected. The answer is yes. The workload expands. The expectations increase. But a week is still a week. If our work/life balance was challenging before the promotion, it becomes even more so after.

Health and families are the loser, and burnout is the winner.

In the endless pursuit of your lifetime employability, where the answer is always yes and more is always better, find your equilibrium. Know your limits. Know what you can do and what you can't do.

Lifetime employability is not always about saying yes, but saying "here's how I can make this work." Taking care of work means also taking care of you.

Beware the Catch 22.

You're never too high in the organization to not seek advice

Ah, the virtues of lifetime employability... increased visibility, leadership roles, and best of all, promotions and more money! Maybe even a "C" level appointment. Maybe even CEO.

The higher you go in the organization, the smarter you become. Right? Wrong! The more responsibilities you assume and the more difficult the challenges.

Lee Iacocca, the flamboyant former CEO of the Chrysler Corporation, called in his division heads for a meeting. The topic: How do we compete against the Ford Mustang?

It was not a meeting to be rate is leadership team and demand that they do better. It was a meeting to seek their ideas. Here was the man known for having created the Mustang while employed by the Ford Motor Company, and now having been hired away by Chrysler, struggled with how to compete with his own creation.

Known for having one of the most creative minds in automotive history, Iacocca was not regarded to be a man who looked to others for ideas. Yet, here he was, before his executive team, saying he needed help.

That meeting, and those that followed, led to the creation of the Dodge Charger, which was conceived not by Iacocca, but by a team of underlings. The Charger didn't match the Mustang in popularity and sales volume, but it gave the Chrysler Corporation a viable entry into the fast growing muscle car market.

While Iacocca was smart, creative, brash and an effective leader, he was not afraid to seek advice. He was not afraid to display his weaknesses.

Moving up the career ladder, especially if it's on the fast track, even with all the qualities of Lee Iacocca, can create the notion that you have to be the smartest guy or gal in the room, without the need to seek advice or validate ideas. Very seldom are the best leaders the smartest. The best leaders are those who can harness the best advice and ideas from others and make them work.

Effective leaders, no matter how high they are in the organization, are very effective at seeking advice.

Remember, the burden is yours. You are on your own.

That may seem like an extreme statement, especially if you are employed by a large company. It is not to infer that you do not have help or resources available to you. It is to remind you that your employer is responsible for telling you what to do. How well you do it is up to you.

There was a time when companies made significant investments in developing and improving the performance of their workforce. That is still true today, but not as it once was. Much of the responsibility for training and developing the skills of their workforce belonged to the corporation. That burden now rests with the employee. Organizations typically teach policies, procedures, and the processes necessary for you to do your job. How well you execute those processes and engage others in doing so, is up to you.

Take advantage of all the training your company offers. But don't assume they are going to provide the skills and attributes to excel at what you do.

To improve your quotients in the behaviors necessary to assure your lifetime employability, consider yourself to be on your own.

Conclusion

DURING THE PREREADING period of this book, readers described this as a book on leadership. While we agree with that conclusion and appreciate that perspective. It certainly is intended to be about the qualities or attributes of good leadership, but that is not all its about.

Others said the attributes or quotients outlined in this book should be standard practices which should be assumed by all employees in any position. That, we also agree. And if they were assumed by all employees, the productivity, innovation and employee engagement in corporations, in our estimation, would shoot through the roof.

The responses we've received are exactly what we would have hoped for. It is about all those things. But ultimately, regardless of your position in your organization, it is about remaining viable and valuable in the workplace and thus, being employable in an ever-changing business climate.

Whether a fresh college grad launching your career, or a seasoned veteran in a major leadership role, we are all challenged to sustain our employability, to maintain our relevance, to remain of value to our employers. And given the pace of change and innovation in technology and competition, those challenges are greater than they have ever been.

There was a time when competition was no more complicated than that characterized by Macy's vs. Gimbels. Today, Gimbels is but a distant memory, having closed its doors in 1987, and Macy's is fighting to retain its vibrancy against the likes of Amazon or Wayfair or thousands of other online retailers who offer the same products, cheaper and more conveniently.

There was a time when company seniority was an attribute, inferring experience and wisdom. Today, if seniority is your primary attribute, it means you are an expenditure on the balance sheet and at significant risk when the next corporate restructuring takes place.

There was a time when technology was the exclusive domain of the corporate IT department. Users were spoon-fed instructions of what to do, how to do it, and further, what not to do. Additionally, many of those users relied on secretaries or assistants to navigate their technology issues for them. Today, technology is the lifeblood of corporations and an assumed capability of its employees.

There was a time when organizations could absorb the expense of retaining their marginal employees or underperforming managers. They could assign them to special projects or other forms of administrative functions to keep them busy. Today, however, the spotlight of accountability shines much brighter. Competition is more intense, balance sheets are more scrutinized and technology is doing more of the work formerly performed by humans. Marginal performance which was once tolerated has become an almost impersonal posture of *perform or perish.*

Those business practices, which were commonplace in the 20th century, are the death knell for employees in the 21st century. Today's business practices are more demanding, more multidimensional, more technology-centric, and continuously changing and evolving.

And the ones who excel in this new climate, be they seasoned veterans or entry-level employees, will have to display a rich diversity of skills, attributes, and yes, quotients.

In your pursuit of leadership, entrepreneurship and employability, we offer you one final lesson, that does not come from the fast paced, technology driven corporate world, but from a very different source.

Before his death in 2008, Major Raghu Raman was an Indian military officer and gave lectures on military leadership. He was further called on to be a keynote speaker for businesses as well.

In one of his keynote addresses, Raman illustrated the ultimate business success can be found not in fast-paced, technology driven corporations, but in what is typically referred to in India as the country's informal, unorganized and marginalized economy and in its street vendors, which reside in the streets of Bombay and other large cities in India and around the world.

These are business entrepreneurs that conduct transactions not in hundreds, thousands, or millions of dollars; but in rupees (the equivalent of $.01). These are business men and women whose success does not yield a quarterly bonus, a new car, or a trip to a luxury island; but the ability to eat that night.

Raman provides a point-by-point illustration of how these informal, unorganized, uneducated and marginalized street vendors achieve and exceed the success criteria of any Fortune 1,000 corporation. From planning, to cashflow, to change management, and return on investment, these lessons of leadership that takes years for MBA students to learn, these businesswise street vendors master in days.

The lessons of street vendors, which can be found in the streets of Bombay, New York City, Brussels, Amsterdam and Mexico City, can be enlightening. Theirs are the lessons of entrepreneurship and lifetime employability, and there for us to learn, and to emulate.

Finally, we end this book the way you will one day end your career. When that day comes, how will you be remembered? *Will* you be remembered?

Will you have made a difference the lives of those who worked for you? Will you have made a difference in their careers? In the lives of their families?

What about your colleagues? Your bosses? And, what about your company? Will yours have been a lasting contribution, or will it blend into the indistinguishable fabric of your company's history?

And your customer? Will they remember you as reliable, professional, and engaging? Or, will they, too, fail to remember any distinguishable value you provided to their success?

Whatever those memories may be, they are your legacy!

The end of your career, however, is not the time to define your legacy. By that time, it will already have been defined. Looking in the other direction, you have no impact on your legacy as it is defined to date. That is already defined. As goes the well-worn phrase, "what is done, is done."

The opportunity that is before you is to ask yourself how you wish to be defined from this point forward.

What will yours be?

Will it be a legacy of getting things done?

Will it be one of 'getting things done, and doing it the right way? By engaging others? By attracting others into your sphere of influence?'

We close by reminding you of something one of our bosses used to say at the close of each of his morning meetings:

"What you do today will determine if you are remembered in this company or not. And what you will be remembered for. Now go get 'em."

What will your legacy be?

The House of Lifetime Employability

The quotients we have detailed in this book, as we proposed in our introduction, constitute what we believe to be your House of Lifetime Employability, consisting of your foundation, your supporting pillars and your roof.

Think of your foundation as your individual *culture*. It is who you are as an employee; as a leader, as demonstrated by (1) your intelligence, or your IQ; (2) your Emotional Quotient, or EQ; and, (3) your ability to learn or grasp new concepts, or your Learning Quotient, or *LQ*.

Think of your supporting pillars as your *resume.* They are your accomplishments or your capabilities, as reflected by (4) your ability to attract others into your realm: your Networking Quotient, or *NQ*; (5) your ability to deliver results, your Execution Quotient, or *XQ; (6)* your ability to discern the various industry segments: your Industry Quotient, or your *InQ*; and, (7) your technology savvy; your Digital Quotient, or *DQ.*

Think of your roof as your *brand*. It is the way you present yourself to others, as reflected by (8) your ability to market or brand yourself, your Marketing Quotient or your *MQ*; (9) your ability to understand and engage the politics of your organization, your *PQ*; and, finally, (10) your personal style or how you engage others—your Style Quotient, or your *SQ*.

Collectively, we put forth these quotients to represent your House of Lifetime Employability. The more you master them the more you are valued and the more you are in demand as an employee, as a leader, and as an agent of change.

If you have not already done so, we urge you to put on your toolbelt and begin constructing your House of Lifetime Employability. You, your employer, your employees, your customers and your family will benefit greatly.

Regards,

Ashok Shah, Dileep Srinivasan, and Ross Kelly